Other Books by Noah Cicero

Poetry
Bipolar Cowboy (2015)

Fiction
The Human War (2003)
The Condemned (2006)
Burning Babies (2008)
Treatise (2008)
The Insurgent (2010)
Best Behavior (2011)
Go to Work and Do Your Job. Care for Your Children. Pay Your Bills. Obey the Law. Buy Products. (2013)
The Collected Works of Noah Cicero Vol. 1 (2013)
The Collected Works of Noah Cicero Vol. 2 (2014)
The Noah Cicero Bathroom Reader (2014)

Blood-Soaked Buddha

Hard Earth Pascal

by Noah Cicero

Trident Press
Boulder, CO

Copyright © 2017 by Noah Cicero

All rights reserved. No part of this book may be reproduced in any form or by any electronic or mechanical means, including information storage and retrieval systems, without permission in writing from the publisher, except for review.

Published by Trident Press

ISBN 13: 978-0-9992499-0-1

Edited by: Nathaniel Kennon Perkins
Cover Photo by: Josh Addison
Cover Design by: Rachel Pfeffer
Proofread by: Sophy Burns

I would like to thank Bernice Mullins, Nate Perkins, Jake Levine, Brad Warner, and Keith Lepak for all the help and support in making this book

Foreword

Noah Cicero has written one of the best books on Buddhism I have ever read. And he's not a Zen master, or a Buddhist priest, or even a scholar of East Asian religions. Rather, he describes himself in this book as a childless, 34-year-old, grocery store bag-boy.

This is as it should be. Buddhism isn't for scholars and priests and masters. It's not a religion. It's for anyone who wants to find a better way. It's practical, it's logical, it's sensible and it's real. Just like this book.

Far too many books about Buddhism get bogged down in scholarly doublespeak. Others are full of far-fetched fantasies. Noah's book isn't like that. It's a real book for real people.

Besides that, Noah is a great writer. The

stories he tells are moving and profound. I particularly liked the story he tells in this book about being snowbound in a house in Oregon with only a book about Bodhidharma, one of the great pioneers of Buddhism, to keep him company. He also tells some good ghost stories in the book.

But what he does even better than that is he makes Buddhism into something actual. Instead of presenting Buddhism as a lofty philosophy or as an exotic religion, Noah shows us how the Buddhist outlook can make sense out of things that defy understanding, and can even help us when there's no way —not even a Buddhist one — to make sense out of things.

I don't like most Buddhist books. People send them to me all the time to try to get my endorsement. But most of the books they send me either straight out suck, or are just too dull and tedious for me to get through far enough to determine whether or not they suck. It was a pleasure to read this one, though.

This is a rare and special book.

- Brad Warner

Preface

I am writing this for no reason.

I don't know if I have a right to write this book, if it is even permissible.

I am not a Zen Master, nor am I a professor with interest in gaining tenure. I'm a 34-year-old, single, childless grocery store bag-boy. In my culture I am viewed as a terrible embarrassment and have in general failed at life. I'm the lowest of the low. I will gain nothing by writing this book. I am doing this only for fun. This is a creative act. I have read some books I have found in stores, enjoyed them, had a moment of therapy with them, and have thought deeply about them. That is all.

1.
Time

In meditation time begins to lose itself. When staring at a floor for hours; hiking up a mountain; singing Kirtans; time no longer matters. In *Being and Nothingness* Sartre writes, "It is necessary to consider our life as being made up not only of waitings but of waitings which themselves wait for waitings. There we have the very structure of selfness: to be oneself is to come to oneself." In Samuel Beckett's *Waiting for Godot* two men sit/stand by a tree waiting for a person named Godot to come, but the person named Godot never comes. This is how the Western world very much looks at life: as a series of waitings. You wait to become a teenager. You wait to get into your twenties so you can have fun. You wait until you get your job. You wait to find your spouse. You wait to have kids. You wait to see the kids grow up. You wait for promotions. You wait to finally own your house. You wait to retire. You wait to get sick. You wait at the doctor. You wait in the line at the grocery store. You wait to finish the book. You wait to start the next book. You wait to get old. You wait for health problems to start. You wait and wait and wait, and the waiting is *you*. When Sartre says, "The very structure of selfness: to be oneself is to come to oneself," he is saying that in Western culture we are defined by how we wait, by what we wait for, by how good we are at waiting. Since we never stop waiting, our very structure is waiting. We are *waiting*, which means we aren't living in the now, we are living in the future. (I do not think everyone in Western culture is stuck in *waiting* though, there are many people who are stuck in nostalgia, stuck in thinking about the past, remembering years long forgotten by the people around them. We all know someone who doesn't really participate in the people around them, who does nothing but daydream about when they viewed life as perfect. They aren't really waiting. They are alive because they are eating, but really they live in the past).

Meditation messes with time. We are constantly preoccupied with time. Our society demands it. When we are little, we are stuck in schools. There is a giant clock on the wall. We spend most of the day staring at it, obsessed with the hands moving. First we have math, then gym, then music, then lunch, each activity marked out by the clock.

The adults don't let us forget for one second that we are growing older, that we have to be prepared, that we have to get things right, that if we mess up our lives, it is over. We have to do everything on time. We have to learn on time. If we miss the time marker, we have to stay in the same grade. If we grow up and don't finish college on time, if we don't meet the right person on time, if we don't get married on time, if we don't buy our first car on time, if we don't if we don't if we don't on time, everything fails.

All this time is a bunch of pressure, always weighing down on us, never letting us relax. We kill ourselves with this *time* bullshit.

I'm not one of those people that say,

"Time doesn't exist." I don't know what that means, and it doesn't help anything.

Time is like this:

You put a frozen pizza in an oven at 400 degrees for fourteen minutes and it comes out cooked.

First, 400 degrees doesn't exist. Scientists figured out how to measure cold and hot, but there is no cold and hot. Cold and hot exist in relation to humans.

Let me break it down more.

Cold and hot do not exist. The way humans judge temperature is based off the relationship humans have with temperature. Metal melts at 2,750 degrees and if temperature was created in relation to metal instead of humans, 0 degrees would probably be 2,750 degrees. Also there is no cold and hot. There is just a temperature. You can't go anywhere in the universe without a possible temperature being measured.

But 400 degrees does not exist. That is a measurement that humans created.

A time span of fourteen minutes does not exist. It is a measurement in relation to the earth spinning and revolving around the sun.

But at the same time, cold and hot do exist. Four hundred degrees does exist, and fourteen minutes do exist.

To say it another way, there are no apples in the world. There are these things that are often red or green, they are roundish, they grow out of trees at the end of summer, you can pick them with your human hands. They fit inside your human hands nicely, you can put them close to your mouth, you can bite them with these sharp white things in your face, and a chunk will rip off. Sometimes they are soft, sometimes they are hard, sometimes they taste tart, sometimes sweet. You can chew the roundish red thing until it gets to a mushy level, then you can swallow it. But there is no apple.

The language we use isn't reality. It is all just a system of measurements made in relation to us, but it works. Language allows us to talk about reality in a good enough way so that we aren't constantly dying of accidents.

Back to time.

Time exists but doesn't exist.

We don't need time when we are hiking. Often the goal in hiking is to reach the top of the mountain, the end of the trail, or the bottom of the canyon. There is no need for time to get to the top of the mountain. The top of the mountain has been there for thousands of years. It will for sure be there all week. When you hike, you just walk along looking at trees and rocks, sometimes sitting by a stream, sometimes seeing a deer or a lizard. You stand and stare. Time doesn't matter. The mountain doesn't care what time it is. Mountains don't have to be at work. They don't have to finish tests or get anywhere. Mountains change at an imperceptibly slow rate in relation to our lives.

During a Kirtan one gets lost in the music, chanting the same phrase over and over again. Amitabha chants work the same way. Time is lost. In common pop songs there is usually verse-chorus-verse-chorus-musical breakdown/solo-chorus-end. The song has a beginning and an end, but in Kirtan and Amitabha chants there is no beginning or end. Time doesn't matter. A person is able to lose themselves in the chant.

Time is the first misery we must understand because it fills us full of pressure. Instead of enjoying the moment we are living or the experience we are having, instead of embracing the current creation, we are demanding that everything conform to our version of time. Time becomes our master. We throw away our freedom and let time rule us in a state of tyranny.

2.
Mental Chatter

We have thoughts, this ticker of information zipping in our minds all day. We are taught that all thoughts matter, that every piece of info our minds shoot at us is real and that we have to be concerned with everything. We are taught that our ruminations matter.

But they don't.

We have thoughts in case we need one.

We have hands in case we need to pick something up.

We have feet in case we need to walk.

We have eyes in case we need to look at something.

We have ears in case we need to hear something.

The mind is a part of our body, just like

the other parts.

The mind doesn't need to be used all the time.

The following is how we often use the mind in a terrible way:

It is a nice boring hour with friends. Everyone decides to go to a store and get corn dogs. Everyone is smiling and happy. You look at the corn dog in your hand, and it triggers a memory of your dead grandpa that you loved very much. You become sad, stop laughing, and start saying miserable things to everyone, ruining the hour for everyone. You do this because you view every piece of mental chatter as important. But really you could have let the thought of your grandpa go through your head and continued on with new thoughts. Instead, you chose to dwell on the grandpa corn dog memory, ruining the good time you were having with your friends. There was another alternative. You could have smiled and secretly thought about the fun times you had with grandpa before mentally returning to the situation at hand.

Our brains are made of meat. Our brains have no interest in facts. Our brains just shoot thoughts out, hoping they help you get around so you don't get into major accidents.

This is a brain's primary focus:

You are driving, trying to get to a new place. Your brain says, "a right on Sahara Avenue and then a left at Valley View Street, then it should be on your right."

You are on a first date. "Okay, comb your hair, put on a nice shirt, which shirt is the best? Okay, the purple looks good. I'll wear the purple one."

You are at work. "The store sold forty five bags of chips last week, the week before it sold fifty. I'll order fifty-three bags this week."

Thoughts concerning partner. "My partner just got a raise at work. I want to celebrate this in some way because they worked hard and I love them. I'll take them to a movie and dinner on Thursday when we both have the day off."

Or creative thoughts. "I think this painting should have more gray. Gray would bring out the blues."

Those are thoughts that lead to concrete happenings in reality. Those thoughts correspond with reality. Reality is being mirrored in the mind of the agent, then the agent makes the thoughts into reality.

Thoughts that don't matter:

Imagining your ex having sex with their new partner.

Thinking about your death when you are twenty-two and in perfect health, like, even thinking about what song should be played at the funeral.

Daydreaming about becoming a rock star even though you know you will never join a band because you either don't play an instrument or have self-esteem issues you have no plan of ever getting over.

Insanely complex thoughts about how you are going to one-up somebody at work.

Complex conspiracy theories on how the world is personally finding ways to make sure your life is horrible.

Remembering someone that died, focusing all your thoughts on the dead person, crying all the time about it, instead of participating in the lives of the people around you.

Ruminating on personal failures that happened years ago and no one even remembers.

Ruminating on how your parents were unloving, but you are 40 and live thousands of miles from your parents.

Ruminating about money and bills. If you can't pay your bills, you can't pay them. If you can pay them, it takes, like, five minutes to write a check. There is no need to think about money for longer than five minutes. I guess you could write out a budget, but how long does that take? Twenty minutes.

These thoughts aren't real. Let these thoughts pass through the head.

Pass right through.

Don't even wave at them. Don't even look at these thoughts. Your brain is just shooting thoughts out. The fun of life is not found in thoughts.

Most of your thoughts are misery.

The joy of life is found in full body experience. That is why swimming or being in nature or having sex is so much fun. These are full body experiences. When a person is in the forest, all five senses are delighted. They're getting exercise, hearing birds and squirrels, seeing beautiful rock formations and trees. They feel soft breezes hit their skin, smell trees instead of car exhaust and garbage. Their whole body is in it, delighting in it.

When you are swimming, your whole body is experiencing the water. Bodies love to float and wiggle around in water.

When you're having sex, your whole body is enthused. The sight of naked bodies, the smell of your lover, your sense of taste, tongues wiggling around on the person you love, whole bodies moving, crashing into each other. The body delights.

Create your own versions of these experiences. I know people who love archery, people who love basketball or soccer or rock climbing or acting. Personally, my body delights in nature, swimming, and sex, and these activities require paying almost no attention to my thoughts. The mental chatter in my mind is very low on the list of priorities when I hike or swim or have sex. My intuition is being used. My body is being used. I'm just having fun.

How many people are there that destroy the simple fun events of life with mental chatter? Maybe you are one of them. Instead of enjoying nature, they bring all their ruminations about life to the trail. Instead of peacefully hiking, they start racing up the mountain trying to one-up you and the other hikers. Instead of enjoying sex, they bring all these weird anxieties into it, or try to turn it into a porn video they once saw, instead of just enjoying the thrill of being naked and together.

When we are obsessed more with our thoughts than real life, it is misery, not only for you but for everyone around you. How are you going to have fun and participate in reality if you won't let go and enjoy what is happening around you?

Your thoughts aren't reality. They are just blah blah blah blah.

If you let go of all the miseries, if you make it through the dark night, you one day end up eating a sandwich. The sandwich falls apart. You smile and put the sandwich back together. You finish the sandwich, then sit there giggling.

3.
Shantideva's Maxim

In *A Guide to the Bodhisattva Way of Life* by Shantideva, Buddhism gives a profound ethical maxim. The fact we don't teach this in our schools and to our children is a great sadness to me. I hope one day this is taught alongside Kant's maxim.

In *A Guide to the Bodhisattva Way of Life* Shantideva says, "All those who are unhappy in the world are so as a result of their desire for their own happiness. All those who are happy in the world are so as a result of their desire for the happiness of others."

When we seek only our own happiness, when we do nothing but ceaselessly run around trying to fulfill our own desires, we are addicts who don't care about anyone else but ourselves. We are monsters who live in a constant state of stress, frustration, and anger. It's almost impossible to be happy as an addict. You want and want and want. The wanting never ends.

When we demand everyone behave like we want them to behave we are constantly stressed out, angry, and frustrated because other people, animals, and plants also want to do their own thing. To want to control everything leaves a person in a constant state of agony because nothing can be totally controlled.

When we demand that life gives us what we want, when we want it, and how we want it, we will never be happy. Life is not here to give us what we want. Life isn't here for any reason. We aren't here for any reason. If you want to participate positively in the course of events, life allows that. However, it isn't going to live up to your demands. You will end up stressed out, angry, and frustrated again.

When we are driven to ultimate life goals, when we are convinced our life goals are more important than the people around us, then we become protective of our life goals at the expense of other people. We are addicts. As

Dostoevsky said, "possessed."

When the most important things in our life are not the people, animals, and plants around us, but our identities, then we will suffer trying to protect those identities.

Selfishness leads to misery. Selfishness is an addiction, and it never ends. Addiction is consciousness racing ahead of itself. Addiction never allows for the person to enjoy and rejoice in the world. Addiction demands future projections at the expense of others.

Shantideva said, "Consider wealth as an unending misfortune because of the troubles of acquiring, protecting, and losing it. Those whose minds are attached to wealth on account of their distracted state have no opportunity for liberation from their suffering of mundane existence."

We cannot afford to spend our days stressed out about gaining wealth: working, competing, destroying the competition, turning ourselves into robots to get ahead, protecting our wealth, worrying about how much money we are spending, counting every nickel and dime spent, yelling at the people around us for spending too much money, worried that we will lose our money.

Existentially, we do not find happiness when we seek happiness only for ourselves because we don't have a self. There isn't anything solid. We aren't a hole to be filled or a house to be built. Our consciousness is endless. As long as we are awake and alive, our consciousness runs endlessly.

So of course we are never completely satisfied.

Because we aren't dead.

Trying to feed the consciousness, trying to get it to stop being hungry, is impossible. Trying to catch up perfectly with life is impossible.

The second part of Shantideva's maxim states, "All those who are happy in the world are so as a result of their desire for the happiness of others."

We exist in situations, usually with other people, animals, and plants. People are all around us. Our family, our friends, coworkers, and strangers on the street and in stores. That is actually your life, being around those people. All we ever have is our relation to other people, the animals, plants, and objects that surround us. But we don't seek happiness there. Instead we seek happiness in the objects we own, in the job titles we have, in the amount of money we have in the bank. We often seek happiness everywhere else but the people around us.

The people around you are your wealth.

If you want to be happy, do something that creates happiness.

Create happiness.

We can all be happiness creators. It isn't hard. Seriously.

How does happiness get created? How is fun created?

Say you are going to work. On the way to work you pick up cupcakes for everyone. You bring the cupcakes to work. Everyone eats the cupcakes. Everyone is happy!

If you are a boss, show the workers that no one is a means to an end. Spend a few minutes every week helping the lowest workers. Ask people how they are doing. Tell people they are doing a good job. When scolding people, smile while doing it. Show them we are all human and it is okay to make mistakes.

Walk the streets with a smile, tell a stranger they have a nice coat. "Cool coat, where'd you get it?" People love that.

If you have kids, think about something fun to do that you too would love to do. Go to an amusement park, play sports in the yard, go swimming, just hang out with your kids. Kids love hanging out with their parents. Kids don't care if it's just walking down the street and back. They love that. The main mistake parents often make is that they avoid having fun with their kids all year, then they bring their kids to Disneyland or Six Flags. But really kids want to hang out with their parents. Kids want to hang out with aunts and uncles. Kids want to do things with adults. Bring a kid fishing or to the park or to the movies. They love it. Kids love to work too. Let them help you with work around the house. Smile while doing it.

If you want to escape misery and depression, find someone to have fun with. There are people everywhere that just want a smile or a friendly face or a non-judgmental person to spend time with.

Your whole life is just going to be spending time with other people.

And we have such short periods of time with people. People come and go in life. The time we have with anyone is precious. It isn't a game. It isn't a joke.

We as humans are not only experiencing, but being experienced. Other people experience us, just as we experience them. We are an experience. We are a roller coaster, a trip to a far off land, a novel. We are an experience for others.

When you are not alone, you are being experienced.

We can create great experiences via friendly acts, by being mindful of the people around us, by listening to them speak, letting them have control, not demanding all of our wants and needs within the context of every situation, by letting the moment happen, by letting the compromise happen naturally.

We really need to focus on cupcakes because humans love cupcakes. What humans usually do is drive to work and think, "I should get cupcakes for everyone." But we calculate the price, and we don't do it. But what does it matter? Every day you have to spend money. Money comes and money goes. Those people don't. Your coworkers are the people you have to spend forty hours a week with. They are your life too. Work is not separate from life. When you clock into work, you don't clock out of life. While you are at work, you are alive the whole time, existing, just as everything else exists.

What does it mean to be friendly though?

Shantideva said, "Acknowledging oneself as fault-ridden and others as oceans of virtues, one should contemplate renouncing one's self-identity and accepting others."

Being friendly is to not be obsessed with one's own identity, with projecting oneself onto other people, but instead letting people be who they are, finding their virtues, and celebrating them. Talking to people about the nuances of their life, their likes and dislikes, letting them talk about their personal history on this planet, letting them share what they know, what they feel, letting them make jokes, sing, dance, and walk the earth, not forcing yourself down their throats. Political ideologues are the best example for this. When extremely political people meet new people, they announce their political beliefs and start yelling at the people around them that they are horrible just for existing. That isn't very friendly.

We have to admit though, a lot of people don't care about other people. A lot of people would never even think the thought, "Should I get cupcakes for my coworkers?" A lot of people live inside a tunnel of their own wants and projections. A lot of people are so insecure from childhood experiences that being the center of attention makes them very nervous. There are people who were taken advantage of in life, and they are afraid kindness might be taken the wrong way, or they might be taken advantage of. Or maybe they grew up completely surrounded by judgmental adults who only cared about their own egotistical needs. There are people with mental illnesses that, for whatever reason, have a hard time just dealing with reality and other people in general. I don't blame dogs for giving other dogs fellatio all the time. I don't blame cats for chasing red light lasers. The world of humans is very complex, but it becomes a lot easier when we let go of our projections, when we stop demanding our rightness, when we let people naturally be people, when we let ourselves have fun.

4.
Resentment

Resentment is the worst thing you can have. It is like holding fire. It will burn you alive.

A discussion on resentment follows the chapter on ethics because nothing destroys our ability to be ethical like resentment. Resentment is a philosophy and a paradigm, and once we adopt it, it encompasses our beings. Recognizing resentment in ourselves and in others is vital to achieving an understanding of what it means to be human. This is because there have always been people full of resentment, and there will always be people full of resentment.

Nietzsche's famous first essay from *Genealogy of Morals* is helpful for understanding resentment.

Nietzsche writes, "The slave revolt in morality begins when resentment itself becomes creative and gives birth to values: the resentment of natures that are denied the true reaction, that of deeds, and compensate themselves with an imaginary revenge."

People become resentful when they can't do things because of outside circumstances, when they have no will to work and practice, and when they have poor self-esteem.

But I also believe this concerns many people who have it hard in life, maybe those with a physical problem or those who are born into a dysfunctional family. People in contemporary American society watch television and see rich people doing whatever they want with their lives, and instead of being entertained they end up just feeling horrible about themselves. Even though statistics show it is very hard even for a person from the middle-class to become a millionaire, poor people blame themselves for not becoming millionaires. Although it is statistically improbable that a person will be as beautiful as a movie star or model, people still blame themselves for not being that beautiful. Even though it is statistically improbable that people will be born with supreme musical or athletic talent, people still blame themselves for not having that inherent talent. People blame themselves for all kinds of things. When people blame themselves they feel insecure, which leads to a low-esteem. This in turn leads to them doing nothing. What Nietzsche means when he says that they "are denied the true reaction" is that a person with very low-esteem is no longer a free active agent but a reactionary creature that lives inside response instead of spontaneous action.

Nietzsche says resentment "gives birth to values." The best example of this is the racist. This is a person who is full of resentment. The racist picks out a race, say Jewish people, and gives them values. This might be that they are taking all the money or own all the banks, etc. The resentful person actually begins creating a value system that allows them to get imaginary revenge.

Nietzsche: "While every noble morality develops from a triumphant affirmation of itself, slave morality from the outset says No to what is "outside," what is "different," what is "not itself"; and this No is the creative deed."

Noble morality in this sentence can be viewed as the way of the Bodhisattva, which is a way of affirmation, spontaneous action, and living in the moment. The Bodhisattva doesn't say yes or no. The Bodhisattva just exists, just as everything else just exists. The slave morality, held by the resentful person, hates the outside world and everything that is not them or disagrees with them. The resentful person often even hates animals and nature. They hate everything. The resentful person loves to tell other people no. People come begging them, "Please change. Please try this new thing. You'll love it." And they yell back, "No."

This viewpoint is really hard to understand if you are a creative person with some ability for spontaneous action because the resentful attitude sounds insane. Why would a person actually get enjoyment out of telling other people no? The resentful person has no interest in taking responsibility for what they do. They hate existing and being seen by other people. Of course, the next question is if they hate existing so much, why don't they kill themselves? Because they refuse to even acknowledge they exist. They don't truly believe they exist, therefore, how can they kill themselves? And they might actually enjoy saying no because in some dark way they get a thrill out of annoying people.

More Nietzsche: "This inversion of the value-positing eye--this need to direct one's view outward instead of back to oneself--is of the essence of resentment."

The resentful person is refusing to take responsibility, to lay claim to their existence, their being, their participation, and its effect on the world around them. The resentful person is doing everything they can not to be seen or looked at. This is why when the resentful person gets themselves into trouble and the world is screaming at them with overwhelming evidence, they seem befuddled and deny that they did anything wrong. They don't believe they exist. On the other hand, the first step of the Bodhisattva is to admit existence and to lay claim to the responsibility existence creates.

Nietzsche: "The man of resentment is

neither upright nor naive nor honest and straightforward with himself. His soul squints; his spirit loves hiding places, secret paths and back doors, everything covert entices him as his world, his security, his refreshment; he understands how to keep silent, how not to forget, how to be provisionally self-deprecating and humble."

The resentful person is expert at hiding, at avoiding truth, at running away from any evidence that might contradict their worldview. As Sartre said in *Truth and Existence*, "I must decide the truth and want it; therefore I am able to not want it." The resentful person does not want truth. They view truth as obnoxious noise that makes them even more angry. Truth is saying yes.

Truth is saying: "Yes, the earth is millions of years old."

Truth is: "Yes, racism is stupid because black people are nuanced individuals that have the same basic fundamental human nature just like white people."

"Yes, global warming is real because experiments and data gathered by scientists all over the world strongly suggest it is."

Truth is saying yes, which is in opposition to the nature of the resentful person. The resentful Christian person doesn't truly believe there were no dinosaurs. What they truly believe in is telling you, "No, the earth is only 5,000 years old" and annoying you. The goal of the resentful person isn't truth, but annoyance.

Thus spoke Nietzsche concerning the philosophy of the resentful person: "He has conceived 'the evil enemy,' 'the evil one,' and this in fact is his basic concept, from which he then evolves, as an afterthought and pendant, a "good one"- himself."

The resentful person views themselves as good, as wonderful, as innocent, as the victim. The resentful person is always the victim because they despise responsibility. They refuse to acknowledge they exist and participate in reality. They believe they are totally good, that no evil can drip from them, that they are above all humanity. They are completely self-imprisoned in total self-righteousness.

Nietzsche on the non-resentful person, on the Bodhisattva: "Resentment itself, if it should appear in the noble man, consummates and exhausts itself in an immediate reaction, and therefore does not poison; on the other hand, it fails to appear at all on countless occasions on which it inevitably appears in the weak and impotent." Then, "To be incapable of taking one's enemies, one's accidents, even one's misdeeds seriously for very long- that is the sign of the strong, full natures in whom there is an excess of the power to form, to mold, to recuperate and to forget."

This goes back to the mental chatter part of meditation. So often in life, we find ourselves in a situation where resentment arises. We see Donald Trump on television: Donald Trump being a billionaire businessman who is ungrateful, talks in gibberish, panders to the worst part of human nature, and in no way shows any desire for spiritual enlightenment. He is a person who preys on people. Of course, we look at that and wonder why the universe would let some lunatic have so much money and us nothing. We might see someone with a nice Lamborghini and think, "Why does that person get that car and I drive a 2001 Cavalier?" "Why does LeBron James get all that speed, agility and stamina, and I get tired after running for three minutes?"

At this moment in my life I'm single, and when I see a couple that have been together for fifty years I think, "Why can't that happen to me?"

Of course we all have resentful thoughts. We have them everyday. This is probably one of the reasons monks of all religions go out into the forest or in caves. In forests and caves there is a lack of stimuli to create painful, resentful thoughts. But the difference between the Bodhisattva and the resentful person is that the Bodhisattva recognizes the resentful thought immediately as it comes and then lets it pass through the mind, just letting it go. As Nietzsche said, "Forgetting it."

If I am staring at Donald Trump and hating him for being rich and more powerful than I am, what am I winning? You don't get anything from being resentful. Just feelings of pain.

I have never in my life heard the phrase, "resentment is a lot of fun."

Thus spoke Nietzsche concerning the Bodhisattva: "Such a man shakes off with a single shrug many vermin that eat deep into others; here alone genuine "love of one's enemies" is possible- supposing it to be possible at all on earth."

The only way of loving your neighbor is if you are extremely forgetful.

We are constantly doing goofy things to each other. Someone gets mad and yells "fuck you." Sometimes our partners cheat on us. Sometimes they stay out too late. Sometimes our kids stay out too late. Sometimes our parents say the wrong thing. It happens. Most people don't wake up with the intention of ruining other people's days. If someone hits you with their car, they didn't do it on purpose. If someone didn't show up on time, they probably didn't do it on purpose. Just forget it. Let it go.

There is a difference between, "I forgive, don't do it again," and, "Oh, I forgot you even did that." Because forgiveness makes you powerful, but forgetting just leaves it somewhere in the past to become a blurry memory.

Hui-neng, a Zen Master from seventh century China had an opinion on resentment. Master Hui-neng hit a student named

Shen-hui three times.

Hui-neng: Shen-hui, when I hit you, did it hurt or didn't it?

Shen-hui: It hurt and it also didn't hurt.

Hui-neng: I see and I also do not see.

Shen-hui: Master, why do you see and not see?

Hui-neng: My seeing is always to see my own errors; that's why I call it seeing. My non-seeing is not to see the evils of people in the world. That's why I see and also do not see. What about hurting and also not hurting?

Shen-hui: If it did not hurt, I would be the same as an insentient tree or rock. If it did hurt, I would be the same as a common person, and resentments would arise.

When we see our own errors, we are taking responsibility. We are admitting we exist, we are free agents, we have choice, and we are participating in the reality that people and things are being affected by our behaviors. But we have to remember adding up the errors of others will not lead to our happiness. If we spend all our days criticizing and hating on other people, when will we find time to be happy, to rejoice, to do awesome things?

Shen-hui said, of course we hurt when we are hit, when we are humiliated, when we have suffered at the hand of others. Of course we hurt. We all hurt when we've been attacked or have been mistreated, and we hurt in very much the same way as others. But we can't cling to the hurt. We can't cling to the pain. Of course there are people who have hurt us, but being obsessed with them only gives them the power. Better to forget.

This is where Jesus fails. Jesus asked God to "forgive" our sins. Instead, he should have asked God to "forget" our sins.

5.
Nothing to Attain

Have you ever felt like you were endlessly chasing something?

The situation we have now is that we are convinced if we just do or accomplish certain things, we will be solidified.

The They teaches us that if we accomplish the specific goals of graduating high school, going to college, getting a job, getting married, and having children, an angel will come down from heaven and give us an award saying, "Good job! You win!!!"

To discuss this in a more nuanced way, say our mother or father doesn't show us a lot of love because they have their own personal problems. Then we spend our adult life trying to accomplish things to make them happy, and we truly expect that one day they will love us, but it doesn't work. They never love us the way we want them to. The chase never ends.

Resentful people think if they tell other people "no" enough, basically torturing their fellow humans, then their lives will be better. But their lives never become better. The resentful person might get a little adrenaline rush from one-upping someone, but an hour later the feeling is over, and they are again existentially left alone with their misery.

Take Fleetwood Mac. They wrote the song "Rhiannon," one of the greatest songs ever made by the human species. You would think after such an achievement angels would have come down from heaven and anointed them with nirvana, then Fleetwood Mac would have turned into beautiful glowing balls of light and just lived in the Divine. But that didn't happen. They all had to keep living.

As long as we are alive, as long as we are conscious, we have to keep living. If we are poor or rich, Filipino or Canadian, if we just wrote a song that will be played for decades, or if we work as a cashier at a Toys "R" Us, or are a drunk homeless person shooting heroin in Karachi, Pakistan, we have to keep living. Our consciousness keeps flowing, desiring, remembering, contemplating the future, hoping, etc.

All my life I was always convinced that if I did the right things I would be successful. I worked really hard in college. I got up early in the morning in Ohio, snow covering the ground, sometimes five degrees outside. I would drive to school in this bitter cold with the car tires spinning and sliding around in the snow. I took out massive amounts of student loans. I did what society told me to do. I got good grades, I made conversations with my professors, I read extra books to learn my subject of interest better. I showed enthusiasm. After college I went and taught English in South Korea with a girlfriend. I worked hard there. I learned the alphabet of the Korean language. I learned several hundred Korean words. I lived in an area of Seoul where I often went days without seeing anyone else who spoke English as a first language. I thought all of this would give me experience to find a job. I thought it would show that I was a winner, a person that succeeds in life.

When I went back to America I had $7,000. I had a million stories to tell. I had everything going for me. In less than two months my close friend had died of cancer, and my girlfriend left me. Then my family said they were selling the house and moving across the country. I had no home. I moved across America and couldn't find a job. I didn't know the town. I didn't know anyone there. I had no ability to network. My money kept depleting. I kept drinking beer and smoking cigarettes. I couldn't find my footing. I didn't know what to do.

I moved to a small town outside Portland with the money I had left. A friend from high school with a good job let me live with her in an A-frame house on an old dirt logging road. It was in the middle of nowhere on a small mountain. I went from living in Seoul, South Korea, the second biggest city in the world, where I had everything--my own apartment, a beautiful girlfriend, money in my pocket, prestige, and friends--to less than a year later being miserable and alone in the forest of Oregon. The wifi barely worked. I couldn't even watch YouTube videos.

I had nothing left. No job, no money, nobody cared about my Korea stories anymore.

It was winter. I began hiking down the logging trail into the forest with a Labrador named Fin. It was cold. I would wear gloves and a stocking cap I purchased in Korea. There was no one out there in the forest, just trees and moss.

I was alone during the days. My friend would work ten maybe twelve hours a day, six days a week. I was left alone in the forest. I would sit and read. I had recently bought a copy of *The Zen Teachings of Bodhidharma* with a Barnes and Nobles gift card someone had given me for Christmas. I read the line, "The truth is, there's nothing to find." I sat there staring at it, saying to myself, "What the fuck does that mean?" No one in my life had ever said such a thing to me.

Then, two pages later, it said, "To say he attains anything at all is to slander a Buddha. What could he possibly attain?"

Things got even more isolating. A terrible snow storm came and trapped me on the mountain for three days. Oregon doesn't have salt trucks because it rarely ever snows to such an extent that it demands them, so I was left there, on the mountain for three days with Bodhidharma.

No one in my whole life had ever said, "There is nothing to find."

Everyone my whole life had screamed at me, "You have to keep moving, access your potential, keep working, fulfill your dreams. If you just work hard enough, you'll attain your dreams." I worked really hard, and ended up just feeling like myself everyday. Being myself never ended, no matter how much I drank, no matter how much I loved, no matter how many job applications I filled out, no matter how many times I showed up to work on time and did my job, no matter no matter no matter, it all just ended with me being me, endlessly waking up with my body somewhere, having to continue.

In the final pages of *Being and Nothingness* Sartre slams down the same conclusion:

> Many men, in fact, know that the goal of their pursuit is being; and to the extent that they possess this knowledge, they refrain from appropriating things for their own sake and try to realize

the symbolic appropriation of their being-in-itself. But to the extent that this attempt still shares in the spirit of seriousness and that these men can still believe that their mission of effecting the existence of the in-itself-for-itself is written in things, they are condemned to despair; for they discover at the same time that all human activities are equivalent (for they all tend to sacrifice man in order that the self-cause may arise) and that all are on principle doomed to failure. Thus it amounts to the same thing whether one gets drunk alone or is a leader of nations. If one of these activities takes precedence over the other, this will not be because of its real goal but because of the degree of consciousness which it possesses of its ideal goal; and in this case it will be the quietism of the solitary drunkard which will take precedence over the vain agitation of the leader of nations.

No matter what we do in life, we can't be

solidified. Our essence is not in ourselves, we are constantly in a state of creating ourselves, constantly in a state of becoming. Heidegger said that the definition of "now" means "in order to." We exist constantly, without remorse, without end, in a state of *in order to*.

In Hindu Mythology, there are gods that stand on a single toe for thousands of years. Just standing on one toe, and thousands of years pass. Then one day they stop, they put both feet flat on the ground and start walking again. It doesn't matter how long you meditate, when you are done meditating you are yourself again, condemned to freedom and to participate in society.

"The truth is, there is nothing to find." As the snow fell in Oregon, I kept reading that line, over and over again. I learned then that my fate was to be: to have this body, to wake up everyday, myself.

A few weeks later I read from Dogen that "A fish swims in the ocean, and no matter how far it swims there is no end to the water." Which is like saying, "A human walks in their mind, and no matter how far the human walks there is no end to the mind." There is no end to consciousness. It never completes itself.

After I read these lines, my mind started to spin and spin. It couldn't hold itself together because every thought I had ceased to make sense; all my thoughts were geared toward accomplishment, consumed with becoming things, obsessed with how other people saw me, obsessed with impressing other people, with attaining personal goals on time, and even being resentful of the world for not giving me what I thought I deserved.

I started hyperventilating, having panic attacks. I started crying, violently crying. I couldn't stop crying. Imagine a 33-year old man crying and hyperventilating on a daily basis. I just couldn't think anymore. I didn't know how to deal with people. I eventually broke down. I lost the ability to speak. I had to be medicated because I had truly lost my mind.

The mind that I had lost was the mind of control because that's what we try to do when we try to attain things. We try to control reality. We believe intensely in doing things that will give us what we want, we demand that situations go our way, we demand that people view us in specific ways. We even demand of ourselves that we behave in a very specific manner. Everything was dreadfully serious. I was serious.

Later on in the book, Bodhidharma says, "Our endless sufferings are the roots of illness. When mortals are alive, they worry about death. When they're full, they worry about hunger. Theirs is the Great Uncertainty. But sages don't consider the past. And they don't worry about the future. Nor do they cling to the present. And from moment to moment they follow the way."

We want everything to be certain, to be locked down, nailed down. I woke up everyday forcing myself to suffer. No one was putting pressure on me. No one was demanding me to worry so much. No one was forcing me to consider the past, to worry about the future, to demand my now go right. No one was doing it but me.

It is really hard to realize, "I might be doing this to myself."

Basically this only works if you allow yourself to admit to yourself the following three things:

You have no real self.

You are continuous.

You exist in the conditional. You arise out of the conditional. You arise, just as all things arise.

As Bodhidharma said, "To find the Buddha all you have to do is see your nature. Your nature is the Buddha. And the Buddha is the person who's free: free of plans, free of cares." You will giggle endlessly. You do everything you did before – go to the bank, go to the gas station, pump gas, call your friends, listen to music, show up to work and do your job – but you will do it not expecting rewards, not expecting to be solidified, not expecting anything to come of it, hopeless but okay with it. And when you walk down the street, instead of your mind swirling around wrapped up in the next new plan to acquire things, you will see the tree leaves flap in the wind. You'll see an old building you never saw before. You'll see children playing. The world will be there, instead of just your goal-oriented thoughts.

"The truth is, there is nothing to find."

6.
Supernatural Thoughts: Ghosts

When I was traveling from Ohio to California in 2004, the car broke down outside of Ridgecrest, California. My friend and I were deep in the desert when the car broke down. My friend began to cry, and the sun beat down on us. A tow-truck driver, a strong young man actually wearing overalls with no shirt underneath, picked us up and drove us and the car to the town of Ridgecrest. The man at the mechanic shop told us where there was a hotel down the road with a pool.

The hotel clerk was a Nepalese man with long hair. He never stopped smiling. He gave us cookies his mother had made. We went to the room and threw our bags down, hoping the mechanic wouldn't charge too much to fix the car. After about an hour of relaxing in the room watching television, we heard a noise from the bathroom that sounded like water rushing into the sink. We both stood and walked into the bathroom, and to our surprise the faucet was turned on full blast. We stood there, just staring at it with what I assume were goofy looks on our faces. I went over and turned the faucet off. Then my friend and I played with the faucet, thinking something must be wrong with it. It seemed to function fine and didn't do anything weird again.

My friend and I went to the pool and had a great time. We felt relaxed and came to terms with the car having broken down. Ridgecrest turned out to be pretty cool, we thought. We went back to the room and fell asleep. In the middle of the night, we awoke to the television on and the volume blasting. We both sat up in bed and, with probably with the same goofy looks on our faces as before, stared at the television being on. Then one of us reached over and turned the television off.

We didn't feel scared. We didn't feel like we were in a horror movie. We didn't expect demons to invade our bodies. We both left the hotel thinking something was odd. If it was only the faucet that had turned on, we would have forgotten the whole thing, and if it was only the television that had turned on, we would have forgotten the whole thing, but since both things happened we began to assume it was a ghost.

My friend and I have stayed in many hotel rooms together, and nothing like that has ever happened again. Actually, never in my life has any other faucet or television ever turned on without human interaction.

My friend and I went to a place called Five Points around 2005. It is a famous haunting site in Northeast Ohio. It is the kind of place where "creepy things" happen. There are haunted train tracks. If you put your car in park, the car will move and fingerprints will be on the trunk. Cars will disappear on the road, and strange noises can be heard. If you put "Haunted Ohio" into Google, Five Points will pop up on many websites. My friend and I decided to go there with a disposable camera and take some pictures. We walked around the area where the creepy things happen and took some pictures, the whole time laughing and having a great time. We are not ghost hunters. We do not believe in aliens or bigfoot or discuss conspiracy theories. We are people with college degrees who never go to church and read a lot of Dostoevsky and Richard Yates. We also happen to watch a lot of horror movies and enjoy feeling scared. So we went to the creepy place and took pictures.

When we developed the film months later, every picture was normal except the pictures from Five Points. Weird red lines went vertically through the pictures. These lines were not present in any pictures taken anywhere else. My friend and I stared at the pictures, probably with goofy facial expressions, and concluded nothing except that it was odd.

Years later, my same friend ended up working in a nursing home in Chardon, Ohio. The nursing home, like Five Points, is now internet famous for being haunted. The nursing home was founded in 1939, and it sits basically in the middle of the forest. My friend ended up finding the job via a Craigslist ad. She had no intention of working at a haunted nursing home.

My friend told me many of the myths surrounding the nursing home. Several strange things had happened, even to her. One night, she was walking by the cafeteria and saw a full-body apparition of an elderly woman eating an invisible meal. My friend is a very logical person and an intense atheist, but is still absolutely convinced that she saw an apparition.

I have just presented three ghost type experiences, but I have come to understand that even if ghosts exist, their existence doesn't imply a moral value system.

The ghost experiences I have had, a faucet and television turning on and red lines in a photograph, do not in anyway supply evidence of Jesus, Allah, or reincarnation. A faucet turning on does not tell me that heaven exists or that there is a god who is watching me. A red line in a photograph does not tell me that Jesus existed 2,000 years ago and he came back from the dead and then flew into space. Seeing an old dead woman in a nursing home in Ohio does not indicate to me that I have had many past lives and will have many future lives.

Ghosts don't imply anything.

I think that religion comes from ghosts,

that weird things like faucets turning on and dead people being seen have always happened. This is where religion starts. Imagine these events taking place thousands of years ago among illiterate people who died by the time they were forty-five. Even in 2015, we have people like the Scientologists, very educated people who believe in aliens. We have politicians who went to Harvard, who don't believe in global warming even though 97% of scientists say it's happening. There is no shortage of people with wacky ideas in our world.

Now imagine people with zero education experiencing something weird like this happening. Obviously, just like us, they will chit chat and make up opinions on why things happened.

What I assumed happened thousands of years ago was that something creepy happened, and humans started making things up.

What I notice, though, is that other-dimension religions like Christianity and Islam do not come until a high level of civilization emerges and some form of societal control is needed. In Judaism, Taoism, ancient Greek mythology, and Navajo and Hopi spiritual practices, there is no demand for heaven. They have local gods who help them with life on earth. Only after an intricate political hierarchy develops, one that requires a massive amount of control to sustain itself, does heaven develop. The Brahman hierarchy demanded a system of reincarnation, the Roman Empire demanded more control in its later years, and the Islamic world saw fit to utilize the other world as soon as it started out.

Heaven is an outgrowth of empire. It is a way for politicians to control the citizens, to keep them in line and hoping.

We have to think about what heaven is. Heaven is a far off land with superior military, judicial, and prison systems. Despite it being a supreme power, governments love this place called heaven. This is precisely *because* heaven always has a stronger military and its prison system is much crueler and harsher than the one on earth. This is really weird. Humans have done a lot of horrible things to each other. We have the means to light people on fire and make them gnash their teeth. We could do that to a person for many decades if we felt so inclined, but we don't. Humans have lit people on fire, but we did it knowing they would die within minutes, and we lit those people on fire as a warning to other people not to commit the same crimes. But, for some reason, we believe that God is great because he would put a human in a place of fire and brimstone for eternity?

Our own behavior, even when we are at our most horrible, has been friendlier than that. There are plenty of historic examples of grisly human behavior. We have brutal ancient empires from Rome to China, we have Medieval torture, and we have brutal 20th Century Dictatorships. The obvious example is World War II. We have clear examples of the horror and agony we can inflict upon each other, but at no point have humans put other people into a room of flames and keep the temperature at 130 degrees while people dressed as demon monsters poked them with pitchforks. Humans generally either kill people immediately or neglectfully let them starve. Often times, when people are doing horrible things to each other, they have been brainwashed into thinking they are doing it for good reasons. There are no good reasons for sending people to hell for eternity. We as humans do not enforce the level of capital punishment that Christian pastors assume God does.

The gods forced Sisyphus to push a rock up a mountain, only for it to fall back when he got it to the top. Humans don't do that to other humans. What humans like to do is enslave other humans into doing labor for them, which is the most horrible thing we do to each other. Strangely, when the Christian and Muslim God punishes people, labor is never put forward as punishment. Probably because the entitled slave masters wrote the books and did not want their slaves viewing their own lives as hell. This is another case of using otherworldly hell as a means of control. The slave owner tells his slaves, "Slavery isn't that bad, because if you disobey God, slave, you will be boiled alive for eternity, which is a punishment worse than my whip."

We have to assume that heaven and hell are political techniques. By creating an invisible, super horrible place that we will go to when we die, rulers gain two unique powers. The first is that governments are allowed to call on this special place to help them defeat their enemies and create new political policies, which convince the masses that whatever the government is saying is true and should be acted on. The second power gained is that governments and the wealthy can now tell their citizens that they are kinder than the gods, that their mercy is greater than the gods. Like a mother saying to her child, " Just you wait till your father gets home."

Empires always make hell worse than their earthly justice system.

7.
Heaven and Hell

Let's pretend we have a soul.
And this soul has consciousness.
The next thing we have to ask is:
What is consciousness?
Let's put it at this bare minimal definition
Consciousness is -

A. It is conscious of something

B. There is a method of interpretation of that something.

Say there is a dog and a human.

The dog sees a tree. The dog is conscious of the tree. The dog interprets the tree to be a place where it can pee. The dog sees nothing but a location to pee. The dog doesn't see a beautiful tree, potential timber, or anything else.

The human sees the same tree. The human is conscious of the tree. The human interprets the tree as timber, or as beautiful, or as a way of building a house, or as a place to build a treehouse for their kids. One human may see the tree and want to cut it down for firewood. Another human may see the tree and believe it is beautiful and should remain to grow old.

Our minds are methods of dealing with information, or what we are conscious of.

Let's go back to heaven and hell.

In this thought experiment, it doesn't matter if we are discussing heaven and hell because both words imply the same thing, that our consciousness pops from this reality into another one.

Wittgenstein said at the end of the *Tractatus* that "the temporal immortality of the human soul – its eternal survival after death – is not only without guarantee, this assumption could never have the desired effect." Just because you pop into another reality, doesn't mean you'll be any different as a person.

Let's take three people.

Jim spends his life chasing after wealth

and power. He spends many hours at work. He follows all the rules. He never shows emotion. When he talks to the other bosses and the owners, he calls the bottom workers low-class, stupid, lazy freeloaders. He votes for politicians who openly say they will pass laws to keep the lower-classes stuck with the lowest wages possible and even stuck without health care. Jim spends his days buying merchandise that makes him look good in front of the other company men. Jim never buys what he wants, only what impresses other people. Jim has actually never for a minute considered what he wants. Jim works endlessly toward a future. He is always saving money. He is always worried about his retirement. He counts every dollar. He checks his bank account on his phone constantly. Jim discriminates everyone by their bank balances and levels of education. When he meets people, he immediately asks them what jobs they have and in which neighborhood they live. Jim never talks to his kids like they are people outside of himself with their own dreams and motivations. He views his kids only as extensions of himself. Their lives should represent him. They should behave and become successful adults like him.

Dave is white and on painkillers and drinks. He has two kids. He works at a factory, making $16 an hour. When he gets home from work he takes a painkiller and sits on the couch watching television and drinking beer. He drinks one after another. Dave never speaks to his kids unless it is to say something horrible, usually a snide remark about how they are slow, how they have no agility, how someone else has better grades at school. When black people or Latinos appear on television, 35% of the time he says something racist. When women show any kind of determination or talk too much, he yells something misogynistic at the television. Dave goes to work and comes home everyday like that for years. He never takes a vacation. He never goes to baseball games. He never sees a new movie. When he hangs out with his friends, he talks about celebrities' net worth, he talks about how someone's daughter got knocked up out of wedlock, how people are stupid. Dave notifies everyone around him everyday how everyone else is stupid and he isn't. If Dave were younger, he would go on the Internet and write horrible comments on YouTube and Reddit about how fat and stupid women are. Dave constantly uses gross generalizations as a form of conversation. Women are this and men are this. Blacks are this and Latinos are this. There is no gray area in Dave's world. Dave never smiles, he never dances, he never feels relaxed.

Jim is consumed with the future and having power. His consciousness never ceases to demand situations go the way he wants them to, and that people fit into his hierarchies. His personal needs and his sense of entitlement outweigh all of humanity; when reality doesn't acquiesce to his demands he gets immediately angry. He doesn't view humanity as groups of different people trying to live their lives. Instead reality is just Jim. Everything outside is hostile. People, animals, and plants are all hostiles trying to take what he has. Jim has to defeat them to maintain and grow his wealth and power. There is no time, no reality for Jim, only his ambition and worries and the endless perilous fight against the hostiles.

Dave is the opposite of Jim. Dave is incredibly insecure. He doesn't believe he is entitled to anything, and because he doesn't believe he is entitled to anything no one else is entitled to anything either. That is why he is a racist and misogynist. If he can't have something, then no one should have that thing. Dave can't have anything because he doesn't believe he can do anything. He is the man of resentment, trapped by his own mind. But at the same time, Dave ceaselessly wants things. Dave is never satisfied. He watches television mentally pretending he is wealthy, or he is a detective or a physicist, who is very funny or owns a bar in Boston. He watches reality shows about people who work on fancy cars, one reality shows after another about millionaires spending their millions. Dave is obsessed with wealth, even though he has no intention of getting any. Dave doesn't even save his money. He buys a house and two cars he can't afford because he wants to look normal in his neighborhood. Dave feels horrible everyday, and all he does is reinforce the misery by watching television.

Now let's do another person, named Lenny. Lenny had a horrible crisis in his mid-thirties. Before that, he used to be like Jim and

Dave. He worked hard and put a lot of pressure on himself, but at the same time he had a lot of resentment towards those who did better at life than he did. He succeeded in many ways, but these successes never made him happy. His partner left him because he didn't spend special time with her, and when she left she took the two kids. Lenny was alone for the first time in his life and was forced to face the choices he had made. He had the choice of sliding into resentment and paranoia, but instead he chose to take on life and accept it as is. He began exercising and eating healthier. He remembered his favorite authors from when he was young, John Steinbeck and Jane Austen, and he started reading them again. He began reading their books, studying them, trying to understand them. Instead of thinking lousy thoughts about himself and life, when he had free time he would contemplate those authors. Lenny joined a local yoga class, where he met new people unlike any he had ever met before. Lenny started watching documentaries and movies instead of just anything on television. Lenny started hanging out with his kids, bringing them places, and while there he smiled and the kids smiled. Lenny started mindfully participating in the lives around him. He laughed and smiled at work. It used to be that when Lenny was at the office, he would complain and complain about how work was stupid and how he couldn't wait to get home. But now he went to work knowing work is part of life, so why not enjoy it even if it is a goofy job? When Lenny saw poor people or the homeless he didn't think, "freeloaders" but rather, "they probably have good reasons." And when Lenny encountered rich or entitled people he thought, "They probably have their reasons too." It isn't that he forgave everyone. He just let people be. He began to feel that judging everyone was just a waste of time and did nothing but cause anxiety and needless frustration.

As opposed to Jim and Dave, Lenny learned to accept life as it is. He accepted the world and its imperfections. He came to learn that the most valuable thing he could do was smile and be healthy.

Let's say Jim, Dave, and Lenny all died and popped into another reality. Maybe this reality was heaven.

Jim would pop into the next reality and demand that everything went his way again. He would want people lower than him, people higher than him, and strict rules to guide his behavior so he wouldn't have the anguish of human choice. What heaven could there be for Jim? There is no heaven for Jim because Jim demands that people suffer for his happiness. Jim would only want to go to heaven so he could tell people he didn't go to hell.

Dave would pop into the next reality and find the nearest couch to sit on. He would sit on that couch and bitch about everyone in heaven and everyone in hell. Then he would watch a television show about people being in heaven, without actually wanting to go to heaven himself. Dave doesn't want to go to heaven or hell. He just wants a nice place to complain.

If Lenny went to heaven or hell he wouldn't even know it (unless he was actually on fire because being on fire makes it impossible to have any sense of enjoyment). But if hell was even a little less than fire, Lenny could find enjoyment. This is because, to go back to the maxim of Shantideva, "All those who are unhappy in the world are so as a result of their desire for their own happiness. All those who are happy in the world are so as a result of their desire for the happiness of others." If Lenny was in hell and saw another person, he would strike up a conversation, make a friend, and find a little happiness. If Jim was in heaven, he would find another person, figure out their social class, and mentally ridicule them. If Dave was in heaven, he would mentally accuse everyone of getting a better place in heaven. He would call the angels something derogatory, complain that angels had more than he did and that humans truly owned heaven, and he would keep on living out his resentment.

If you want really wake yourself up:

Imagine living for eternity with your current shitty attitude about Being. Really imagine it. What if you had to live for eternity with your current shitty attitude?

8.
Reincarnation

Let's pretend reincarnation is real, that something about us does not cease at death, that something about us has existed always, or at least for a very long time. Let's even say that the universe made some weird soul thing, something at the quantum level that doesn't die but continues finding new organisms to live in.

I've chosen not to use the Hindu version of reincarnation. It just reminds me of political science. Hindu reincarnation basically states that how you perform your duty during one life leads to your station in the following life. This just reminds me of Christianity, Islam and Mormonism in which there is a heavenly judicial system weighing on cases on every single organism in the universe. We die. Then we go before a court of angels or devas, and lawyers come and provide evidence on everything we ever did in life, and the judges make a ruling. Then we get shipped off into another body or accepted into heaven or hell. There is nothing natural about that procedure. It seems ridiculous to assume that there would be heavenly courts, judges, and lawyers. *The Tibetan Book of the Dead* takes on a more natural version of the human soul.

(As I lay out the basic ideas in *The Tibetan Book of the Dead,* experts on Tibetan religion will probably note I am not staying true to the text. I am not including fornicating otherworldly beings and such. I am trying to distill the essence as much as possible because I do believe there is great value in understanding reincarnation as a thought experiment.)

Imagine you have a soul.

A little blue glowing light, not in your head, but in your heart. Your heart is what keeps you alive. The heart dies and your body ceases to function. You aren't just your head, but all of you. When you feel agony, your heart beats wildly. When you are making love, your heart beats wildly. Your heart sends blood to your genitals making them strong and full of life.

This little blue glowing ball lives in your heart.

When you die, when your heart stops beating, the little blue glowing ball leaves your body. It floats above you.

Then, depending on your mental state, the glowing ball directs itself to a new a place.

Where it will go depends on your attachment and aversion.

We must understand that attachment and aversion are the same thing.

If we are attached to cigarettes, we have an aversion to not having them.

If we are attached to our children, we have an aversion to them getting hurt or being taken away from us.

If we are attached to the idea of ourselves being seen as smart, we have an aversion to ourselves being seen as stupid.

If we are attached to being the boss and having power, we have an aversion to being in a position without power and doing the bottom jobs.

If we are attached to being seen as tough, we have an aversion to being seen as weak.

If we are attached to our lives, we have an aversion to death.

Where you find attachment, you find aversion.

And this is where the agony resides in us.

We are almost constantly in a state of maintaining and protecting our attachments. We get up everyday, we open our eyes and immediately realize we are ourselves again. Unless something very odd as happened, we wake up in the place where we went to sleep. We wake up, get out of bed and begin the protection of the day. We go to the job that we feel best represents how we want to be seen. We work in a way that describes how we want to be seen. We buy specific merchandise that tells the world how we want to be seen. If we don't like how we are being seen, then we do things to get out of the situation. We go to schools or change jobs. While we are at the job we don't want, we tell everyone at that job we are going on to do bigger and better things. We complain. We look sad. We make ourselves sad. Instead of enjoying the time we have with our coworkers, we complain. We tell ourselves in our minds, silently, that our coworkers have settled for less, they aren't hard workers like me, they don't have what I have.

The more you have, the more you have to protect.

You want a house, you have to protect it.

You want kids, you have to protect them.

You want a partner, you have to protect the relationship.

You want a car, you have to protect it.

You wants lots of money, then you better be ready to protect all that money (In my opinion most people do not strive to become rich, not because they aren't hard workers, but because they can intuit that wealth often makes life excessively complex and burdensome).

For most people, their lives arise out of the need to be constantly protecting and maintaining the objects they have, the objects they want to have in the future, and their identities, or how they want to be perceived.

Now imagine doing this charade one life after another, over and over and over again.

Shantideva said, "Countless eons have

passed away while you sought your own benefit. With this great toil you have gained only suffering."

Go sit somewhere where you can people watch. Now see. Look!

These people walking by, all in states of protection, driving themselves crazy with trying to maintain the pretenses of their local traditions. Now imagine them doing this over and over again for thousands of years. They are born 856 BC, they live out the stress of that world, then they die, then they are born again in 768 BC and live out the stress of that world. Then they are born again in 601 BC to live out the stress in that world, and then you see them in the local mall. They are buying shoes they think will make them look cool. They are buying a shirt they can't afford. They are screaming at their children. They are complaining about prices. They never sit down and just look at the mall. Their minds are racing from one marketing stimulus to the next.

(Now, I want to say I like malls. I like new shirts, but I don't buy shirts based on other people. I buy what I like, what strikes me as awesome.)

Imagine all these people doing this routine endlessly for eons and eons.

To return to attachment and aversion, in Buddhism one lets go of attachment and aversion. They find a middle way between the two. Of course, Buddhists, just like everyone else, have strong feelings toward other people. They get up and do things to make sure they have shelters. They get up and do things to keep their jobs. They have children and prefer that nothing bad happens to them. The difference lies in understanding that everything changes, that things are changing right now as you are reading this.

The difference lies in this:

The person full of attachment and aversion says, "I'm going to get this job, I'm going to marry a partner that looks like this, work this specific job and get promotions, then buy a house, have this many kids, live in this area. I'm going to wear these types of clothes, drive this type of car. I've started a retirement fund. When I retire, I'm going to sell my house for this much, then move to this place. My kids will graduate high school, then go to college, then become successful adults."

This type of thinking can lead to a lot of trouble because life doesn't offer perfection. This type of person will get up everyday demanding perfection from society and everyone around them, and when things don't go their way, they will find scapegoats who they will blame for their life not being perfect.

The Buddhist kind of mind says, "I'm going to go to college because I am 20-years-old and life is long. I might as well go. After college I will find something else to do. Because there is nothing else to do, might as well do something. I will try to find a job I like because if I do a job I like, people will see my sincerity and will probably appreciate it. If I lose my job, I will throw a fit for a week and then look for another one, but I don't expect society to maintain my job for the entirety of my adult life, which is 40 years. That is a bit much to ask. In my forties or fifties, I might have to learn new things. I don't know what those things are yet because I am only twenty-five, but I do know that the world is changing, and for sure in twenty-five years the society I live in will probably have a different economy than it does now. I will meet people and love them. I will hope for the best in every relationship. If the relationship fails, I will learn from my mistakes and be a little different in the next relationship. I will have children, but I won't pressure them to be straight or to conform to certain roles. If they don't go to college, or if they want to do something really wacky in life, I will go along with it."

The difference is that a person consumed with attachment and aversion is convinced they know everything, when actually they know nothing.

The Buddhist mind accepts it knows nothing. It doesn't even want to know anything. It has no interest in knowing because even trying to know is needless stress.

The Buddhist mind says, "I think that if I do these things these other things might happen, but I don't know. I don't know what will exactly happen, but I do know that if I force everything to happen how I want it to happen my mind and body will become filled with bad feelings."

There is a great story in the Tibetan tradition about letting go of attachment and aversion.

Marpa, the Translator from Tibet, goes to India to visit Naropa the great Indian guru. At one point, Naropa is in a cave eating a human. Naropa has disemboweled the human and is eating the intestines, ribs, and brains of this human corpse. Naropa offers Marpa the Translator some ribs, but, disgusted by the act of cannibalism, Marpa the Translator refuses to eat them. Then Naropa says, "If you do not enjoy this as great bliss / The enjoyment of great bliss will not arise." Naropa and the corpse disappear. Marpa the Translator sees that remnants of the dead body have remained behind. Marpa the Translator then licks the remains and feels great bliss.

Think about like this. If we live life after life after life for eternity, we are going to enter into many situations we don't want to be in. We are going to find ourselves, life after life, in situations where we feel great agony, where we basically have to eat another human, or where we have to eat the feces of animals,. And why do we feel this agony? Because we demand that things go our way, because we thought things were going to go one way and they ended up going another way.

Naropa basically said to Marpa the Translator, "Let go of everything right now. Never demand again. In any situation, no matter how horrible, look at it with a smile. Recognize the impermanence. Recognize that you don't know anything, and let things happen."

To return to *The Tibetan Book of the Dead,*
You die.

Your body is lying there. Other people are there, but they are living. They are taking care of your body, probably moving it somewhere where other people don't have to look at it.

A little blue glowing ball has left your body. It floats above you.

Imagine a person named Debbie has died. Debbie has lived to be 75-years-old. Debbie is angry all the time. She hates how society has changed. The doctor says Debbie shouldn't eat salt, but Debbie eats salt anyway. The doctor says if Debbie walks for a half an hour a day, then her legs will feel a lot better. Debbie won't walk. Instead, she sits and watches television. The doctor wants Debbie to eat more fresh fruits and protein, but instead she lives off of instant meals and powdered donuts. When Debbie's family brings her healthy meals to eat Debbie laughs and says, "I don't care. I like salt."

Debbie always complains, telling every young person she encounters that getting old is terrible. She never jokes. She never spontaneously does anything. Everything she does is a reaction, and her reactions are so predictable that everyone can easily imitate her behind her back. Debbie never does anything with anyone. She never participates in the lives around her, but at the same time she makes constant demands of the people around her. She wants them to help her, to take her places because she no longer drives. When her children drive her places, she doesn't ask them about their lives, but demands that her children listen to her complain about her life. When her children try to tell Debbie about things happening in their lives, Debbie just waits until they are done speaking and resumes her complaining.

When Debbie dies, her little blue light will float above her. The little blue light will become very confused and probably terrified at being outside of a human body. Debbie's little blue light will want salt and powdered donuts. Her little blue light will scream, "Give me powered donuts!" Then her little blue light will travel around trying to find a fetus to be inside of because it naturally can intuit that bodies are required for the intake of salt and powdered donuts. There is no nirvana for Debbie because she doesn't want nirvana. She believes firmly in her desires being fulfilled, not peace and relaxation. Debbie is firmly attached to the earth.

Take the case of Joanna. Joanna is 82-years-old. She spends her days complaining about how her grandkids are worthless. She talks about how one of her grandchildren has married someone from another race, how another grandchild is lazy and makes no money, how another grandkid is a drug addict and no good. Joanna complains constantly about how society has changed for the worse, how there are too many minorities, how she doesn't walk the streets anymore because men of other races might rape her. Joanna never goes to new restaurants, she never listens to new music, she is always commenting on how young women dress like sluts. She watches hours upon hours of television shows that reinforce all her fears and paranoia. When her children visit her, she tells them their kids are horrible. She says horrible things about the neighbors and generally disapproves of all humanity. Her psychology is that of a person bouncing from one fear to the next. Joanna is attached to all her aversions and to her own identity of being a white woman living in America. She grows angry at the world for not respecting her whiteness any longer. When Joanna dies, her little blue light will be very confused. Her little blue light will want a new fetus, a new home where she can scold the world, where she can keep fearing.

Joanna has no self-awareness. She hates humanity, animals and even plants. She has never for one second in her life taken a walk alone and reflected on how she affects other people's lives. She views reality as an extreme duality. It is Joanna verses all of the earth. Everything is her enemy. She doesn't know her mind is just a chatterbox. She thinks every thought she has is real and important and objective, but actually she lives in a world of extreme subjectivity. She feels good when negative things happen to other people because when bad things happen to other people it justifies her existence. Joanna has lived a life ruled by The They. She has never taken control.

Imagine Joanna dead, her little blue light floating above her body. Will Joanna see heaven? Could Joanna even see heaven if it was right there in front of her? I believe her need to feed her resentment would lead her back to the earth to find another fetus, in order to keep feeding that resentment. She is used to it. She is used to fear. In heaven there is no resentment. There is no fear. Heaven would probably feel horrible to Joanna. A world with justice would make Joanna feel incomplete. Joanna, in her current mental state of resentment and fear, would find that world incomprehensible and therefore very frightening.

Tracy is another person doomed to die. Tracy is 76 years-old. Tracy, in most people's opinion, is kind of weird. Tracy is retired and lives in a small apartment. She loves her little apartment. She has decorated it with pictures from the entirety of her life. She has pictures of her late husband, children, and grandchildren, of course, but she also has knickknacks she picked up from her travels. During the course of her life, Tracy made it to forty states, where she purchased many funny postcards. Tracy likes to sit and look at the postcards, smiling, thinking about the trips she took with her family. She has little knickknack statues and teapots she bought from Europe and China when she went to those places (Even though Debbie and Joanna made approximately the same amount of annual income as Tracy, they never traveled outside their country. Wealth had nothing to do with Tracy's travels). Tracy often sits, looks at the statues, closes her eyes, and re-lives the entire experience in her head.

Tracy always helps babysit her grandchildren. Tracy likes to bring her grandchildren swimming and to the park. For hours upon hours, her grandchildren will ramble about doing kid things, and Grandma Tracy plays with them as much as she can in her elderly physical state. Tracy feels immense joy around the children. Tracy loves to see the children experience new things, to become conscious of the world just like she did when she was little. She doesn't just want to see her own grandchildren, but the human race continuing. Tracy sees no-duality with the children. The children feel excited to experience new things, just as she felt excited when she was young to experience new things.

When Tracy's granddaughter went to the army and had to do desert training, she asked grandma for special snacks from a health food store. Tracy drove out to the health food store and bought as many snacks as possible. She told every worker at the store, "I'm buying these for my granddaughter!" Tracy's whole body always becomes full of pride when her children and grandchildren accomplish things. Tracy's pride is not earned in a specific way. Tracy always takes some time to think about everyone, to get into their heads a little. If her grandkid Charlie loves cars and machines and doesn't show any signs of going to college, she doesn't yell at Charlie to do better in school. She lets Charlie be Charlie, and when Charlie graduates from electrician school, she throws him a party. When her grandchild Kristin gets pregnant at age nineteen, Tracy doesn't yell or accuse her of ruining her life. She merely says, "Life is long. Each thing will sort itself out as time passes." Then she smiles at her grandchild.

Tracy never stops listening to new music, reading new books, or watching new movies. She even watches professional sports sometimes. Tracy loves to see that young people are doing exciting things, that the human race will not end with her. She feels happy and secure in the idea that when she closes her eyes for the final time, the human race is still alive, still having fun, making new music, playing sports, having political arguments, making mistakes, fixing them, making different mistakes, realizing some mistakes can't be fixed, and in general living out a very similar life to the one she has had.

Because of Tracy's relaxed attitude, she has often been mistaken for dumb, timid, and childlike. Tracy never really had a lot of friends. When people talk, they often speak in judgmental terms, but Tracy doesn't find judging other people in harsh terms enjoyable. She doesn't like talking about people in bad ways. She likes to talk about other people in terms of getting inside their heads, trying to figure out why they do things, which in her opinion leads to the best way of helping them. But most of the time people don't want to talk about that. They want to simply talk about other people based on their appearance, which Tracy never enjoys.

Tracy never worries or talks about money. Her basic philosophy is that if she and her husband went to work and worked reasonably hard, then money would happen. She doesn't spend a lot of money because she doesn't really want much, but when she spends it she doesn't look at receipts or count pennies. She feels being miserly is boring. When things go wrong, like her kids acting up, or people being mean to her at work, she doesn't hold grudges. She doesn't talk shit. She doesn't find ways to retaliate. She waits a while, then politely says, "Hello, how are you?" and smiles. She just forgets about what has been done to her. Of course at times she thinks of it, but she knows the answer is not to dwell. She knows that most people don't wake up with the intention of hurting other people. People get angry sometimes and do mean things in the moment, but when the moment is over so is their anger.

In her last days, Tracy spent her time at

the community pool in her apartment complex. She would sit in the pool by herself or sometimes with her grandchildren. Children of every race would swim and scream in the pool, black, Latino, Asian, and white, all together in one pool screaming, throwing balls, dads on the side of the pool smiling, moms holding tiny babies introducing them to a pool for the first time. Tracy couldn't stop smiling at the sight. She knew when she was little, in the 1940s, nothing like that could have ever happened. She believed the world was going in a beautiful direction, and she hoped she had participated in a way that made it a little better.

Before Tracy went to sleep at night, she knew she might die, she took some deep breaths, and said, "If I die tonight, it is okay, I've done what I could with what I had."

When Tracy dies, her little blue light will float above her body, but unlike Debbie and Joanna, she won't feel such an attachment to the earth. Her easy going attitude prepares her for anything. Instead of feeling confused and terrified by the experience, Tracy might feel, "Wow, this is exciting!"

Tracy feels that the earth is okay. She doesn't feel a stubborn resolve to keep eating certain foods or to keep feeding her bad feelings. She accepted life, and then she accepted death. Tracy naturally has heaven or nirvana. She *let go* of the earth.

Buddhism prepares one for heaven. Unlike Christianity, Islam, and Mormonism, which view heaven as a contest in which people are born and perform a lifelong series of duties that are necessary to enter heaven. Capitalism works the same way. In capitalism, people are expected to perform at work, network, and believe in themselves, and eventually capitalism awards the market warrior with millions of dollars, creating heaven on earth. If you are not a millionaire, then you should at least respect and adore the millionaires, buy their products and not join a union. If you follow the rules, then the millionaires will grant you a job and a house, and you will maybe not attain full heaven, but a second tier heaven. You will be able to physically see the bottom 80% of society that live in hell, and are therefore demons.

(The bottom 80% don't actually live in

hell, most of them laugh, have families and do fun things all the time, just at a cheaper rate, but the top tier people like to rationalize that the bottom lives in hell, because it justifies their existence.)

Christianity, Islam, Mormonism, and Capitalism all believe in duties, in doing specific acts, and in not doing other specific acts. Buddhism teaches that, as Bodhidharma said, "According to the sutras, evil deeds result in hardships and good deeds result in blessings. Angry people go to hell and happy people go to heaven. But once you know that the nature of anger and joy is empty and you let them go, you free yourself from karma."

There are no duties in Buddhism. The main focus, if there is any focus, is to let go of allowing extreme emotions to take over, to let go of holding on too tightly.

Anger comes. Let it go.
Happiness comes. Let it go.
Fear comes. Let it go.
Boredom comes. Let it go.
Sadness comes. Let it go.
Sentimentality comes. Let it go.
They are just moods. Moods come and go.

Moods are formless.

Of course, it feels powerful to be struck by anger or humiliation. It is a whole body sensation. For me personally, the terrible feeling can last for hours, but I know it is just a feeling. Tomorrow I will feel something else.

The basic premise of preparing for heaven is:

You can't do things to get merit to escape reincarnation.

You can't not do things to get merit to escape reincarnation.

You have to learn to do and not do things without letting those things consume you.

9.
God and Coyote

God.

When we discuss God, we always throw our projections on God.

We make God what we want God to be.

I will now take my turn and make God what I want God to be, and maybe you will enjoy it or you won't.

About five years ago, I was driving through Oklahoma at sunset. I could see for fifty miles around me. The fields were endless. It was hot and the sounds of the cicadas were intense. The sun was huge, the biggest sun I'd ever seen, and there it was setting over those giant fields. I felt at that moment, looking at that sunset, "There is God."

Many times I've taken these three children

fishing. Their dad had become a crack addict and run off. The children were fatherless. I would take them fishing. They seemed happy sitting on the dock, playing with worms, impatiently waiting for their bobber to get sucked under the water. They seemed excited and full of life, and I thought, "There is God."

When I've met women I soon after fell in love with, when I felt their kiss and embrace for the first time, when we spent time in bed together, giggling and smiling, I thought, "There is God."

When I see people protesting for their rights, after being trampled on for decades, sometimes centuries, I think, "There is God."

When I hear stories of men storming the beach of Normandy, watching their friends die next to them in a hail of bullets, still persisting because they knew they had to stop the Nazis, I think, "There is God."

Not it terms of there being a God in heaven, but *there it is*, right there, for all of us to see. But what am I seeing? What is the relationship between falling in love, protesting in the streets, and storming the beaches of Normandy? The relationship is courage.

To me God is courage, the will to try something new, to do the unpredictable, to let go and then to take chances you have not taken before, to attempt to persevere even though the world is telling you no, to leap into a world of uncertainty.

The sunset is like seeing The Grand Canyon, a little bird singing on a branch, the mountains of Colorado, playing fetch with your pet dog, endless beauty that fills one full of awe, and that awe is God.

Sometimes though, I say "There is no God," when I see people who live their lives with no self-awareness, with no desire for enlightenment whatsoever. When I see people who are full of resentment, full of self-loathing, who worship prestige and wealth, who think trolling people on the Internet is somehow going to make their lives better, I think, "There is no God." But I do not mean no God in heaven. I mean, when I look at that specific thing, that specific mindset of resentment that hates uncertainty (because if courage is embracing uncertainty then cowardice hates uncertainty), when I see people who refuse to the embrace the uncertainty of life, who desperately want their life to remain the same at the cost of other people, I think, "There is no God."

When the coward sees something beautiful and, instead of letting it remain beautiful, wants to blow it up for the sake of money, there is no God there because the coward feels no awe. The only thing they feel is their delight in destruction.

Our biggest projection concerning God is that we want an explanation for what has happened to us and to the people we love. A lot of us humans want to die and confront God. We want to scream at this Being, "why did you do this to me? Why did you give this to another person and not give it to me?" The idea of asking God *anything* could be the most pointless use of emotion ever invented. What benefit could possibly be derived from that?

Let's say, just for a second, there is a God, there is a Being located in another dimension. This Being has created this universe. Let's say this Being has created many universes. Science kind of tells us now that there are many universes, so what if one of the other universes created this God? As in, their evolutionary path led to the creation of a God, and this God figured out how to create other universes. And this is our God, this Being that lives forever in another dimension, and this Being is watching us and has the power to direct our lives? What does that mean? Why would a Being of any kind do that? Why would a Being of any kind create an alternate dimension? And then put little wiggling creatures on random planets? Why would this universe have more stars than humans? Could the universe actually be made for stars? Does God also love stars?

What if the universe was made for frogs or ants?

What if the universe was made for comets? Comets are cool.

I can't logically deduce anything on why a Being would create an alternate universe and then fill it full of stars, then have the stars explode, and eventually after billions of years little wiggling organic creatures show up that are made of stardust but look nothing like stars, then the god living in the other dimension would notify the wiggling creatures on two legs via prophets of a god living in another dimension.

Two Proofs of God I have made up for fun:

A. *The universe produces no duplicates*

One object cannot perfectly replicate itself. If the universe has any design, it is perfectly designed to *not* perfectly replicate itself. Because it is the imperfect replication that gives us a sense of space and time.

What is I mean is this:

In the forest it is obvious no two trees are the same. When an orange tree gives birth to hundreds of oranges, no two oranges are the same. When an orange seed gets planted, the tree never looks exactly like the tree it came from. When looking at a gravel driveway, there are no two identical pieces of gravel. Humans and animals have given birth to millions of animals, and the children always look slightly different than the parents. Even with machines designed to create identical parts, even though when we look at the parts and they look identical to the others, when we look under a magnifying glass or a microscope, we can see that even machines can't produce exact duplicates.

And think about time. Right now it is

9:40 a.m. Pacific Daylight Time on August 16th, 2015. At 9:41 a.m. Pacific Daylight Time, the world will be completely changed. Even the universe will be changed. Everyone and everything will have moved just a little bit. The entire history of the universe abides in 9:41, but nothing remains of 9:40. No two minutes are identical. The universe strangely seems incapable of producing duplicates.

B. *Energy demands consumption and holes.*

Black holes are giant eating machines that sit at the center of every galaxy. The organisms on earth eat oxygen and food. All the bugs, animals, and plants are all eating each other. Plants eat the nutrients out of the soil, the herbivores eat the plants, the omnivores eat everything. As I sit here typing, there are microscopic mites on me eating my dead skin and bacteria in my stomach living and helping me digest food. The universe has given birth to different forms of itself, which then need to eat each other to gain energy to keep wiggling about. But the universe probably doesn't care because the universe remains the universe the entire time. If a lion eats a zebra, the universe is the lion and the universe is the digested zebra.

Then the lion poops and the zebra becomes fertilizer which feeds more things. Wherever there is a hole in the universe, something is meant to go in it or go out of it, which is odd because it looks like the universe had the intuition to create holes and tubes. How would the universe know to create holes?

I don't know if the creation of holes implies intelligence, but it implies intuition. In the same way a house cat has no self-awareness and often seems totally indifferent to us, the universe is totally indifferent to us but at the same time has an innate ability for intuition.

But overall, proving the existence of God or intelligence is useless. God does not clean my kitchen or take out my garbage. God doesn't pay to fix my car when it is broken. I do these things, or people I know do these things.

Bo Jackson, considered the world's greatest athlete, once said in an interview that he had "God-given tangibles." These were that he could run fast, had great agility and hand-eye coordination. Believing that our tangibles are God-given seems okay with me because if I say "God gave me the tangible of philosophy," that means I have something without having earned it. If I practice and work hard, I could turn that tangible into something great. Therefore, I should practice and work hard because God gave it to me. I shouldn't be arrogant about my God-given talents because God gave them to me. I didn't earn them. Because God has given me these talents, I should share them with other people, and if any of these God-given tangibles makes me wealthy, I should share my wealth with others.

I believe there is a difference between a person saying, "The Pennsylvania forest looks magical in October, the colors of the leaves are so beautiful. I feel overwhelmed with some sort of ancient spirit among these trees." and someone else saying, "I hate homosexuals because my pastor says the bible tells me to!!!"

My mother, who goes to church, has said to me, "I pray to 3,000 angels for you to get a better job." I seriously don't think 3,000 angels are listening to her pleas and if there are angels watching over my life, they probably have a better idea of what I need than my mother does. But I don't scold my mother and tell her to stop doing that. I understand that she is saying, "I hope you get a better job." She is merely expressing concern for me.

Several years ago, I went to the funeral of a close friend. He was slightly Christian in that he liked to read the bible, he went to church randomly, etc. but he didn't believe in the new order of hating homosexuals or being anti-abortion, so he went to the church and remained quiet. Because of his years at church, a lot of Christians showed up to the funeral. Several of the Christians went up and spoke. They didn't really talk about him. They would stumble over a past life event and then read a few verses from the bible. It hit me then that most people aren't articulate, most people don't know what to say, they have feelings but no words. They resort to the bible because they've been told all their lives the bible has words that mean things. They read sentences from the bible and try to make themselves and everyone else feel better.

When it comes to God, the most important thing is giving up on the idea that God is on your side and not others, that if you perform specific duties God will honor you and not others. Because the logic of this is very odd, the religions of Christianity, Islam, and Mormonism describe a God that lives in another dimension, and this God is angry all the time. This God's anger never ceases. This implies something very weird. I believe most people have a very hard time grappling with the fact that if they consider the implications for even a second they will see that a God has created a universe to make himself angry.

Why would a God create another universe from scratch to annoy itself? That seems insane.

I did not add the Jewish God into this because the God of the Torah is a local God, like Coyote or Spider Grandmother. The Jewish God is a God that lives within the boundaries of the Middle-East, that hovers above the Jewish people, watching the Jewish people. The God of the Jewish is like a grumpy old grandfather who wants the best for his grandchildren, who is scolding everyone to act right and do a good job at work. The God of the Jewish people reminds me of my dad scolding me to clean my car, yelling, "People who have respect for themselves clean their car!" "When you meet someone, stand up straight, smile, speak clearly, and shake hands with a firm grip." "Read the directions twice before you start." "Take notes in class." "Make friends with the right people." The Jewish God is mostly about factual human behavior, the basics of getting along in a civilization.

It was the Christians and Muslims who turned the Jewish God into a Being from another dimension, then gave that Being heaven and hell and an absolutist sense of justice.

Coyote.

Coyote is a god of the indigenous people of the American West. Coyote is different than most Old World Gods. Coyote teaches about life via tricks. Coyote isn't here to save you. Coyote doesn't promise heaven Coyote isn't going to send you to hell. Coyote is going to trick you.

The Jewish god also does a tricky thing in the story of Joseph. God has Joseph's brothers sell him into slavery, then Joseph works really hard and becomes a high ranking official. Years later, his brothers are starving. They go to the nearby kingdom for food, and they end up finding Joseph. But Joseph doesn't get angry. He chooses to forget about the whole slavery thing, and he feeds his brothers.

There are similar themes in *The Odyssey*. Odysseus is thrown around by the gods. Odysseus can't get a break, all of his men die, his boat is destroyed, one problem after another. He returns home and all these guys want to have sex with his wife and take his money, but Odysseus doesn't give up. H persists and gets his house back.

Life is full of tricks. Right when we thought something was supposed to happen, it doesn't happen.

We were convinced our marriage or relationship would last forever, then boom, the other person announces it is over.

We are convinced that going to college, spending all that time in class, doing all the work on time, and getting good grades will lead us to getting a good job right after school. Then, boom, nothing happens. You don't get a good job. You are worse off than when you were in school, because now you still have a badly paying job but no student loan money.

We are convinced our children are going to be great athletes, and we know that if they persist they might actually have a chance to get into professional sports or at least a college scholarship. Then, boom, the kid announces they want to play guitar and listen to Jimi Hendrix alone in their bedroom.

We are convinced our child is going to go to be a great college student. We have been daydreaming about it since they were born. We have spent hours upon hours helping our child learn math and science. We are absolutely convinced this is true. Then one day we get a call from the police station and find out that our child is addicted to heroin, and our child doesn't care at all about going to college.

You are convinced your romantic relationship is completely over with someone. You've forgotten them, they've forgotten you, everything seems over and done with. Then you accidentally see each other at a movie theater. You look into each other's faces and fall right back in love, and this time it works, because you've both changed since the end of the relationship in ways that have made you more suitable for each other.

You are let go from your job. Maybe the place closed, maybe you got fired, and you are convinced your whole life is over. Everything you have worked for was for nothing. But then, a few years later, you are okay again. You don't even think about what happened. Life has moved on.

Life is a trickster party. Coyote is always running around setting up tricks for us, showing us, in the most fun ways, that we are never right about anything.

Think about it like this: somewhere in the future at an unknown date and in an unknown location, you will be proven completely wrong, your life will be greatly disrupted. You will convince yourself you can fix it if you just do these specific things, but it won't work. Something else will fix it, something you've never expected.

10.
Pascal's Wager

The idea of Pascal's Wager comes from Blaise Pascal. In his book the *Pensées* he describes a scenario in which a person must bet between living the Christian life or being an atheist. Pascal is a Christian, so obviously he wants you to bet on Christianity. He says it is better to bet on the Christian life because there is an "infinitely happy life to gain." To him, betting on Christianity has a better payoff than betting on atheism.

An atheist bets only on one earthly life, but a Christian bets on lives both on earth and in heaven: "Let us weigh the gain and the loss wagering that God is. Let us estimate these two chances. If you gain, you gain all; if you lose, you lose nothing."

However, I am not specifically interested in that exact wager, but he goes on to say "Yes; but you must wager. It is not optional. You are embarked. Which will you choose then?" You cannot escape the wager. Every moment of your life is haunted by this wager. The fact you are alive thrusts you into the wager.

That may be so, but the idea of a bet that's only between Christianity and atheism bores me. I've decided to make the bet more complex for our contemporary lives because to me Pascal's Wager represents the fundamental question. For Camus the fundamental question was if we should commit suicide. For me, the most powerful philosophical question is, "What paradigm should we bet on to help us best experience life?" The bet is crucial. If you lose at roulette you can always get the money back, but if you bet wrong on Philosophy you could end up living a life of bleak stupidity.

Let's be honest. Let's not play any games. We've been playing games for thousands of years, and they are stopping right now. No more games.

We all die the same deaths. It doesn't matter if you are a Muslim, an extreme atheist, or you are living in an untouched tribe in the jungle, we all get the same death.

Simple empirical observations indicate that, most likely, death is the end of consciousness. Maybe our consciousness pops into another reality but, as stated before, there is nothing about ghosts that clearly shows us what this other dimension wants. If we do pop into another reality, we have to experience that reality with the same behaviors and attitudes we had in our earthly life. So the crux of our otherworldly jump is still our responsibility. It depends on our ability to respond to the new situation.

This is the truth.

These are the facts:

The only thing that ever happens to us is that we experience reality.

Everyone else and everything else we encounter experiences us.

We have to wake up everyday feeling like ourselves.

We experience reality via our mind and body. We experience reality via our interpretation of reality.

This is the wager.

This is the question.

How are we going to experience and interpret reality?

But why choose the concept of *wager,* or *bet,* or *gamble*?

Because we are free. Each moment is new in its freedom. We aren't solidified. We don't have extremely concrete selves that cannot change. A free person makes a wager. They bet that these behaviors will lead them to somewhere they want to be and then maintain whatever they want. When our lives enter into a crisis, it is often because we were winning many hands, but then suddenly, out of nowhere, our luck ran dry.

Betting is freedom. It is choice. How we bet is our responsibility. The consequences of the bet fall on us. And also, like a game of poker, we have good days and bad days. Sometimes we win, and sometimes we lose. Sometimes we come out even. But a master poker player keeps on playing, and even when they lose everything they keep returning to the table. However, unlike in poker, we are condemned to the table.

We have four basic ways, in these times,

within the North American way of interpreting reality.

The religious view.
The non-theist view.
The Ayn Rand view.
The Spiritual view.

You have to make your bet. You have to pick your view.

I'm going to describe each view because you might already be picking one and not know it.

The Religious View.

The religious view is that of self-righteousness and resentment. The religious person views reality in terms of hierarchies. The religious view discriminates. The religious mind always says, "this is this and this is that. I am this and you are that." The religious mind demands everyone believe in the same thing that the religious mind believes in. This is why proselytizing is fundamental to the religious worldview, because religious beliefs are based not in logic, but in irrational ideas that pander to the fears of human beings.

Religion is anti-logic.

Religion demands that everyone believe in a single belief system.

Religion has a beautiful way of winning arguments.

When a rational person uses logic against a religious person, the religious person doesn't have to respond. They merely send the rational person to hell.

This is why Judaism and Buddhism are not religions. They don't need to have new converts, and they don't feel the need to send non-believers to hell.

When you are religious, when you view reality in hierarchies, when you spend your days discriminating against others and mentally sending them to hell, when you wake up everyday and force yourself to follow strict rules of pretense, when you live out a ridiculous pantomime of a Being from another dimension, you won't feel good.

You will wake up feeling a lot of pressure every day. You will wake up full of hate because others won't believe what you believe. You will wake up everyday hating the present moment because you believe that the earth is horrible and heaven is beautiful. You will wake up everyday having cognitive problems because reality is not actually dictated by your religious view, but by the laws of science.

The religious view *demands*, the religious view wants everyone to behave a certain way, the religious self-righteous person is in a constant state of mental and physical agony because the world they live in won't behave. The religious view does not accept the world.

(I want to state here, because this could easily lead to confusion, that we as humans don't have to accept everything. If there is a political policy that is unjust and making your life horrible, protest. If you want to dress nicer, work some more hours and buy a better outfit. If you want to look more fit, exercise. Accepting life for what it is involves having the attitude of, "I'm not going to demand everyone agrees with me. I'm not going to demand perfection from life. If I go somewhere and some little thing goes wrong, I won't flip out and throw a fit." You would think this isn't a big deal with humans, but everyday I see reasonable adults with white collar jobs and children flip out because, "I've driven all the way to the grocery store and you don't have any strawberries!!!" They just let this mood of anger and misery infect their bodies and contaminate all their feelings.)

The religious feel angry all the time. They are predominantly terrified of the world, assuming that their God will grant them protection from other people God also created.

The religious mind is a tense place to be. There is hardly any fun, just a lot of pretense, fear, and judgment.

There is also a lot of projection. Religious people project themselves onto everyone. They look at other people and project onto them what they think they should be doing. The religious view wants everyone to behave just like them. They think everyone wants the same things out of life as they do and they can't stand behavior that confuses them. It must be acknowledged that this is very hard for people to let go of. Most people think they know what is best for other people, but if you look around the world you will see that people are very different from each other, and often times it is inexplicable and okay that they are different. I know people who never drink alcohol. They drank alcohol a few times in their teens and they didn't like it, and they never did it again. I personally like to drink, but never more than a couple times a week, and months of my life have gone by without drinking. Both are different ways of viewing alcohol, but I don't think either way is a big deal worth talking or thinking about. I know people who never got any higher education and got jobs at grocery stores, factories, and restaurants. They worked really hard and became managers and now make really good money. I know people who went to college and earned high grades and now spend their days working as servers because they just didn't care about becoming white collar. They liked college but didn't like the white collar office world. Neither groups are evil. They are people doing different things. I have friends who haven't eaten meat in years, and I have friends who only eat meat once a week, and others that eat meat in one meal a day, and of course I have friends who eat meat in almost every meal.

For some people, certain things just click. For others, they don't. And I can't honestly figure out what makes one person click a certain way and another person click another way. A lot of people have some homosexual desires and some homosexuals might have some straight desires. When they fall in love, they fall in love with a specific gender, and I know straight people who wouldn't mind a romp with someone of their same gender sometimes, and I can't explain that either, and I feel fine with that.

This kind of open thinking is like, "You know, people are kind of *funny*. Hell, I'm kind of *funny*. My cat is *funny*, that tree over there is *funny*, my government is *funny*, everything is kind of *funny*." I think what I mean by "funny" is something close to "absurd," but not quite. Instead of something having no inherent value, funny is when we can't predict behavior, when it is just inexplicable why something behaves a certain way. We know we do it. We can make statistical graphs on it, we can talk about it, but we don't know the big why, and if it isn't destroying the very structure of society, who cares? Predatory loans and carbon emissions are way more detrimental to society than homosexuality or women who want to breastfeed their babies in public.

On the other hand, the religious view hates funniness. The religious view sees any deviation from the norm as an attack on their God and their lives. Nothing is *funny* with the religious view. Rather, as Sartre noted, everything is *serious* with the religious view. There is no *funny*, there is no irony, everything is deadly serious. The religious view is that heaven is serious, rules are serious, everything you do and say are serious, there is no room for mistakes, there is no room for being a *funny* uncanny human. This is where the inquisition came from. When people get super serious, when they stop laughing and taking things in jest, when they stop smiling, when they stop allowing their fellow humans to deviate, they get serious, and everyone who doesn't take their worldview seriously is guilty. The serious person views themselves as the lifelong victim of everyone who won't take their shit seriously.

This is the bet of the religious view:

Do you want to live a life in which you have to take everything extremely seriously, in which you are constantly criticizing everyone around you, in which you are constantly criticizing yourself, in which you have to wake up angry every day because other people refuse to believe in what you believe in? If this is what you want, then be religious.

The Non-Theist View.

The non-theist view has always been around. We love to say things like, "Everyone in 1240 Europe was Christian," or, "everyone living in Muslim countries is Muslim." Yes, statistically they were and are, but most people, the masses in general, are not deeply concerned with philosophy. They are busy with their families, and work, and are shoved around by the elites. They often live by the mercy of others, and just accept their state and try to live within the rules they are given.

I mainly want to talk about the North American non-theist and how they live their life.

Basically, a non-theist is a person who never thinks about religion or seeks spiritual enlightenment or philosophy of any kind. There are times in their life when they seek advice but they are not extremely concerned about where the advice is derived from. (Note that a person might have lived the first thirty years of their life as a non-theist and then had a powerful moment and decided to pick a new wager. There is nothing permanent about any wager. We can pick new wagers at different times of our lives). They don't care about being rational. Whatever their boss says, they think is true. If someone confident comes along and tells them something to believe in, they just believe in it. They think confidence is a sign of intelligence, even though the biographies of most intelligent people often tell stories about deeply insecure, reclusive people who lacked confidence, and it was their lack of confidence that often drove them to learning more.

I am consciously choosing not to call non-theists "nihilists," even though it appears they believe in nothing in particular. They do often believe in family, they do often believe in protection of their things. They often believe in personal ownership, in the holidays and traditions of their local culture, etc. They just don't have an obsessive belief in religion or philosophy.

The non-theist is the person of the They.

Whatever is going currently, they believe in. They want to be current, they want to be normal, they want to be seen as a well-adjusted individual.

In the 20th Century, the non-theist finally got the religion they always deserved. They got television shows. Television shows – from soap operas to game shows, from sports to sitcoms to reality TV – reveal to us the world of The They. These shows pander to people who are not deeply concerned with religion or philosophy.

The non-theist looks to shows to find out what they should be talking about, what they should be thinking about, what they should look like, how people might be perceiving them.

Non-theists are often insecure. They are afraid of 'going for it.' They don't always do what they want with their lives, because they want to remain normal and part of their personal social division. The non-theist doesn't like to take risks. They get anxiety quickly in unfamiliar situations, but at the same time they want to be the person who takes risks. They want to be the smart person that solves problems or the athletic person who slam dunks the ball or uses their muscles and agility to win the fight. This is what television and marketing plays off of. The non-theist comes home from work and looks at the television screen. The television runs image after image and scene after scene of people who went to Harvard or MIT, people with way more wealth than the non-theist viewer, people with elite fighting skills, people who are more attractive than the viewer is. If they are not a straight, white male and they still want entertainment, they have to watch shows that don't have people who are the same race or gender or sexuality as them basically all day. The essence of television shows is to make the non-theist feel horrible about themselves. By featuring mainly attractive actors, television makes them feel ugly. By showing people who went to Ivy League schools, it makes them feel stupid. By having people with superior white collar jobs, it makes them feel like their jobs are horrible and pointless. Characters in television shows often have grandiose expensive places to live, they have great cars, they have wonderful outfits. Most television shows are designed to justify lavish wealth and make the watcher feel horrible and self-loathing. The average television show leads to self-loathing in the non-theist, and then the television show is interrupted with commercials notifying the watcher of what they don't have, yelling at them, "Haha, you don't have this, other people have this, you won't be normal unless you get this. Aren't you afraid of what people will think about you? Be afraid, hate yourself: you're ugly and subnormal."

The non-theist doesn't know what to do besides repeat banal platitudes about "bettering oneself" or "keep trying" or "don't give up" or "stay positive." Banal platitudes lead nowhere. They help for about three hours then fade out.

The mindset of the non-theist is one of staying busy, staying entertained, never allowing themselves to self-reflect or meditate in silence. They are consumed by the world of entertainment. They have to be entertained constantly. They are at work and complain all day then race home and turn on the screens and let people living in far off cities create art for them. They, like all humans, want to have a voice, so they create opinions about television shows and sports athletes, who will win and who will lose. They spend hours upon hours creating opinions concerning things that have nothing to do with them. Many people probably don't even know what movies or music their kids like, or how many people live in their town. There are several mountains surrounding Las Vegas. We see them everyday, but the locals have no idea what the names of the mountains even are. Yet, for some reason, these people have huge constructed opinions on what rich people are doing in far off cities, on sports teams, on actors they will never meet, etc.

The non-theist will often resort to conspiracy theories, aliens, and other weird things like the Illuminati to consume their time. The non-theist wants a God that requires no morality. They want God but no philosophy. In the mind of the non-theist, aliens are an alternative to God. Aliens are watching us, just like God. Aliens are out there, flying around our planet, watching and investigating us. Aliens provide the feeling of not being alone in a vast cosmos. People seem to have an extreme desire to not be alone.

The Illuminati conspiracy theorist can't accept the chaos of human history, that governments are made up of people like everyone else, and that things happen in a kind of weird chaotic uncertain manner. Believing in the Illuminati gives meaning to history. It gives sense to the nonsense of human direction. It also provides the feeling that at least *someone* is watching, that some people somewhere are in control. It removes responsibility from the individual. A person can say, "Human history is not my fault. The Illuminati did it."

The oddest development in non-theist life is that television and the internet have given them an alternate reality where their minds live. Previous to the 20th Century, humans lived locally, they grew up most likely on a farm, they worked the farm, they went to the closest village to shop at the market, attend church, maybe go to a dance. After they got married in their late teens to early twenties, they moved to a farm a few days away by horseback. They knew everyone in the area. They knew the local forests. They knew the local landmarks. They spent an incredible amount of time living in close proximity to animals and plants. The local world was their world. Their consciousness, the chatterbox of their mind, consisted of local things and interactions. But now, people are thinking about whatever television shows tell them to think about. They aren't thinking about their horse and how much they want to ride it tomorrow, or how they need to weed the beans, or if Arthur Smith is going to become betrothed to Ashley Horton. The non-theist spends their days thinking about athletes they will never meet and if a certain television character will ever have sex with another television character.

I don't know if this new version of consciousness is better or worse than the old version. Maybe it matters, maybe it doesn't, but I don't know how a person could live a fulfilling life being deeply concerned with people they don't know and places they will never be.

Ayn Rand View.

Ayn Rand is a writer from the 20th Century. She wrote books of philosophy about how being selfish is a virtue and doing whatever one wants is awesome, even if it is at the expense of other people. Her basic belief was that trickery was the highest form of ethics, that the apex of human genius is the ability to trick other people into giving you money and power when you don't deserve it. According to her, power is the best goal for everyone: a philosophy that promotes endless desire and clinging, the antithesis to Buddhism.

The Ayn Rand view of reality is a harsh place to be. It is full of paranoia, anger, frustration, the need for dominance, the need for protection, the need to maintain, the need to constantly show no real emotion; a world without jokes, irony, empathy, imagination, a world that doesn't make any sense, a world full of contradictions, a world of endless stress, desire and dissatisfaction.

The Ayn Rand person has a basic problem. In order for them to feel secure in themselves they need others to suffer. They don't feel happiness or calm unless they know that their happiness or calm is coming at the expense of other people's rights and happiness.

It is easy to show this using the example of a wealthy business owner. The wealthy business owner utilizes their business to destroy nature in someway, maybe they are destroying trees for paper, maybe putting giant oil rigs in the ocean, mining beautiful parts of the world, maybe forcing animals to live in horrible conditions, and then after the animal lives in horrible conditions it gets butchered and sold as fried chicken or bacon. Maybe the business owner finds a peaceful forest, looks at the cute little forest, and then bulldozes the whole thing and makes it into suburbs for the wealthy members of the community. Maybe the wealthy business owner drains all of the toxins from their factory into a local river, a river that has been there for generations. Maybe the business owner closes down the factory in its original country, then moves it to a country with cheaper pay and tears up their environment too. Maybe the wealthy business owner goes to another country, a country they don't live in, and destroys the rivers and forests there because their own country won't let them anymore.

And that's just the nature side.

The business owner opens factories and stores and pays their workers as cheaply as possible. The local government demands a minimum wage of eight dollars an hour. Even if the company knows it can afford to start workers at a higher wage, it still only pays them the minimum amount. When the minimum wage becomes too high, the company moves the factory to a foreign country with an even lower minimum wage. The Ayn Rand view is always crush everyone and rejoice. The Ayn Rand person enjoys laying off his long term employees. The Ayn Rand person enjoys the idea of people going home and telling their family that they've lost their income. The Ayn Rand person gets excited at imagining people crying, knowing they will soon lose their house, that their lives are falling apart. The Ayn Rand person loves the idea of having destroyed something beautiful.

The Ayn Rand business owner loves the idea of their workers struggling, of not being able to make ends meet, of making sure that people never get ahead in society. They want to force everyone into buying their products, but at the same time they want the poor masses to struggle for every purchase.

To the Ayn Rand person food, clothes, car

rides, and furniture are all better with blood on them. If they know human suffering and tears have gone into producing their banana or gasoline, they love it all the more. The Ayn Rand person wants the world punished. Absolute control is everything to them.

This reveals itself in the fact that business owners have access to economists and sociologists. They are available. They are easily located and emailed at universities. Business owners could email and ask, "What would be best for my workers? Should I pay them more? Should I pay more taxes? Should I donate to the local high school?" Instead, what we see are wealthy business owners paying the lowest wages possible, doing everything they can to destroy unions, paying millions upon millions of dollars to politicians to ensure the masses always vote against their own interests, and that legislative policies and court rulings always favor the most wealthy members of the population.

The middle or lower class Ayn Rand person is similar to the business owner, but they don't have a huge business. They instead work themselves to management. They are that person who thinks they are too good to wash dishes or operate a machine at the factory. They say things like, "That's below my pay grade."

The middle-class or lower-class Ayn Rand person so badly wants to be powerful that they will tell themselves any lie.

Basically this is how it works: an Ayn Rand person reaches a level of lower management. They start making about $14 an hour. A politician wants to raise the minimum wage to $15 an hour because statistics show that the productivity of the workers does not match what they are getting paid, which means the business is basically stealing wages from the worker. The Ayn Rand $14-an-hour manager will vote against the minimum wage hike because the person psychologically demands that some workers only make eight dollars an hour. The Ayn Rand person psychologically needs someone else to suffer for their happiness.

Now, we know these numbers are arbitrary. Minimum wage workers could be making $10 an hour or $11 an hour, but the lower manager requires that they make at least $5 more an hour than the worker. It helps them sleep at night knowing that someone is suffering, that someone has less food than them.

What the Ayn Rand person wants most of all is the destruction of freedom. They want absolute control over everyone. They want to restrict everyone via low pay and what they can afford to purchase. They want people to be conscious only of them and their products. Because that is what we all are, workers and consumers. Workers and consumers are actually the same exact people, but they've tricked us into thinking we are consumers, not workers. They want the workers and consumers of humankind to be trapped in some ridiculous matrix where the wealthy are seen as beautiful job-creating Gods and, because they are seen as Gods, these business owners are given permission to do anything they want.

The cruel person, that person who goes out of their way to create pain in other people, animals, and plants, knows what causes pain in other people. Everyone knows how to be mean. Everyone has had mean things said to them, mean things done to them.

An example:

A person named Adam says, "Noah, your face is ugly."

This is what happens, and I assume the same thing happens to you.

I feel upset.

What does "upset" mean?

Upset means that I was in a good mood. My mood was steady. It could have been happy/excited/productive etc., but I wasn't sad or depressed or angry. Then someone says to me, "Noah, your face is ugly."

My mood immediately switches. I begin to dwell on what Adam said to me. I keep thinking, "I can't believe Adam said that, I hate Adam, Adam is so mean, is my face really ugly, am I ugly, I want to beat Adam up, Adam is going to get his, Adam has problems, is my face ugly, etc. etc." I feel horrible. I have a terrible feeling mood.

What has happened?

I have become obsessed with Adam. I am focusing all of my consciousness on Adam. Even if he does not have the ability to articulate or understand what he did, Adam can intuit that being mean causes a disruption of mood. Adam knows that calling me ugly has made me become extremely conscious of his Being.

Meanness is about control, about disruption of moods, about creating bad feelings in other people.

But why does Adam choose meanness?

Because Adam is resentful of humanity, Adam doesn't feel good about life, Adam doesn't accept life as it is, Adam feels weak inside, Adam believes he has nothing to offer the world, Adam feels jealous of other people. Instead of accepting all the different people in the world, Adam is convinced that the different people of the world have a conspiracy to ruin his life. Or if Adam has always lived in a position of affluence he might feel completely entitled to do whatever he wants, and he does not see people from the lower economic classes, other races, different cultures, and other genders as fully human, like he is. Adam might view other people as animals, and these animals should be subservient to him and his needs.

When a person is being mean to you, they are trying to control your consciousness.

It must be understood that Adam's mind is

extremely busy. It is bouncing from one paranoia to the next because the Ayn Rand mind is completely terrified. It is a mind that is constantly in a state of protection. Anything that threatens their little world must be violently attacked. Anything that aims to disrupt their desires is violently attacked. Ayn Rand people are obsessive planners. Anything that disrupts their plans is violently attacked. Ayn Rand people hate sharing. They view all sharing as being attacked, which means they have to violently attack back. Ayn Rand people have to tell themselves that all poor people, and often other races, are lower and more violent than they are (even though they are the ones who start the wars), so they say things like, "bad neighborhood" or "Don't go there. It is dangerous" in relation to areas where poor people and people of color live. The Ayn Rand person has to stay convinced that they are genetically superior. They deeply enjoy any lies or political pandering that leads to the idea of genetic and or spiritual superiority, as in God loves them and protects them more than other people. They love the idea of Grace.

I think that a lot of people adopt the

Ayn Rand mindset because, growing up in a country like America, they are inundated with images of wealth. Adults constantly tell children that earning the most money is a sign of genius and greatness. People like Steve Jobs, Bill Gates and Michael Jordan are held up as examples of extraordinary greatness. The best get $$$.

$$$ = Greatness, God's Grace, genetic superiority, and the effects of a well-lived past life.

Television, movies, commercials, and other media outlets notify children on a daily basis that wealth is greatness, and to be selfish is a virtue. Being concerned with poor people, the disabled, the unfair treatment of women and minorities, animals, and nature are signs of weakness. Real men don't care about other people. They care about making money. They are focused on attaining power and achieving their goals, showing dominance and gaining a reputation that demands respect.

You don't become district manager by pushing for raises for your employees, or feeding the homeless that live in the parking lot. You become district manager by making sure the merchandise gets sold, by cutting wages and hours, by kicking the homeless out the parking lot to live in tunnels underneath the city.

Spiritual View.

The word "spirit" comes from the Latin *spiritus* which means "to breathe" or "wind." This is evident in the word "respiration." Also, in the Navajo religion people are "wind eaters," and when a person dies, the wind leaves them. If you stop and think about it for a minute, we are wind eaters. Breathing is a form of eating the wind, and it is the wind that swirls around in us, that gives us life and our wiggling power.

To be spiritual is to learn how to breathe.

To be spiritual is to breathe.

Breathing brings us back to the original moment, the moment we are living in, the now.

Breathing in and breathing out, letting yourself exist.

Letting yourself exist without having to dwell on the past and worry about the future.

What else is there to do besides breathe?

The spiritual wager to me is the best course of action because it allows oneself to live peacefully, to enjoy the life you have, to take advantage of each day. That is all we get. We get days. We go to sleep and wake up to new days, and we have to be conscious, we have to experience the day, but how are going to experience the day? How will the day experience us?

I have formulated a small spiritual plan, which might be a worthwhile wager. It might not, but this is my wager.

I have no heaven to give anyone. I have no escape from reincarnation. I have only the possibility of more fulfilling experiences. This plan doesn't require talent, it doesn't require superior intelligence, and it doesn't require money. It only requires concrete choices.

I have no magic and no love to give. Only loose forms.

Be more local.

In North America, and in much of the world, we have allowed ourselves to get lost in screens. We care more about what other people are doing across the world than what is happening right in front of us.

We aren't centered.

We aren't even where we live.

How do you live where you live?

First you research the history of your place. Libraries are full of books on where you live. It doesn't matter if you are new to the city. If you live somewhere, you live there now. It is yours. You own it. Learning about the history of your location will teach you that you are part of human history, and if you realize you are part of human history you realize the place you are not only has a history, and a present, but it also has a future. The history of your location will inform you how to best participate in the future of your location.

Learn the mountains of your area. Learn what animals and plants live on those mountains. Drive up to those mountains on your day off and try to find some of those animals and plants. Spend some serious time with an old tree. Sit next to the tree. Lean on the tree. Touch the tree bark with your hands. Put your face on it. Find old rocks in the forest, sit by the rocks, talk to the rocks. Look up where the ponds and lakes are. Find out what kind of fish swim in them. Find out how those fish got there. Look up landmarks. Find the oldest building in your town and walk around in it. I've stood next to the Empire State Building, seen the stars in Hollywood, visited the Palace of the Governors, seen the Redwoods in California, touched 4,000 year old bristlecone pines in Nevada, and hiked to the bottom of the Grand Canyon to learn the heart of my country.

Going to local places and learning about one's country is good not only because it gives a person a sense of their place in human and geologic history, but because it gives us something to do, and that's what we really want. We want something to do. And this is the choice. You could choose to play more video games, watch more television, or troll on the internet, or instead you could go online and find neat things to do in your own area. This will give you something fun to do, something worth remembering, something to make you feel alive for a second.

In reality, there are a lot of fun things to do. There might be a small lake in your neighborhood. Go there and sit with a friend. Walk down to the river and look at fish swim by. Go to a local museum you've never been to before. Go to the dirt track races in a rural area. Go to a restaurant that serves a kind of food you've never eaten before. Go to a local blues or country music fest. Who cares if you don't listen to that music? Just go. Have fun. What is it worth being so obsessed with your identity?

Pick out a few books.
Find a few books or authors and read them over and over your whole life, studying them, thinking about them. Personally, I have read the works of Dostoevsky and Sartre over and over again since my late teens, and lately I have come to love Bodhidharma and Hui Neng. These books give me nourishment. They give me something to think about because the mental chatter never ceases. We have to fill that chatter up with something. What better way than with a book that teaches us about life, a book written by someone who has thought intensely about life.

My high school principal, the man who taught me so much about reading, would read

Henry David Thoreau's *Walden* and Ralph Waldo Emerson's *Self-Reliance* every year. He would teach these books to his senior students with total joy in his heart.

One of my friends reads Kate Chopin's *Awakening* and Jean Rhys' *Good Morning, Midnight* repeatedly every year. She loves to dwell on Chopin and Rhys. She loves to read their biographies and discuss them at length.

A Buddhist friend I have reads Dogen. He has read everything about Dogen and loves to dwell upon Dogen's words. He has even gone so far as to write books about Dogen.

Having the same books with us our whole life not only helps us through life because of the lessons offered in the books, but it provides a constant. Our lives will change dramatically as the years pass. As we enter into new stages of life, we sometimes forget what we were about, who we used to be, but these books bring us back. These books can give us that feeling again, the feeling of being young, of being confused, of wanting to learn what life is about.

Before I began writing this book, I bought a copy of Edgar Allan Poe's short stories and poems. He was the author I read when I was thirteen who first inspired me. I reread some of the poems and short stories, trying to remember why I wanted to write in the first place. I had forgotten why I wanted to write. Often in life, we start things with great enthusiasm and energy, we are inspired, we are full of life to make things happen, and we have the best reasons: passion and love and the desire to contribute to the world of happenings. But then we get caught up in money, responsibility, fame, wanting to impress people, wanting the promotions, and the original driving force is lost. And that is when we start to suck at life, when we lose the original love.

Be forgetful.

There is no use in clinging to the past. Remember the past, but don't cling.

Pretty much all of us have had something terrible happen to us. We all have been humiliated, we all have done stupid things, we have all had injustices done to us. We have all had mean things said and done to us, but it never helps to cling to those horrible things.

Once I had my heart broken, and I refused

to let go. I cried and cried, I drank alcohol, I threw fits, I wouldn't get a job, my mind was totally lost. The other person was gone. She had moved on. She didn't live on my side of the country. She had other things to do and think about, but instead of just letting go I kept thinking about it. I kept forcing myself to get up everyday and dwell on the past.

I wanted to know like a petulant child.

Why did she leave?

What did I do wrong?

Why was I so stupid to trust that person?

Why wouldn't she ask me to come back and love her?

What aspects of me caused her to leave? I needed to know those aspects so I could change.

Why is my love not good enough for anyone? Is there something wrong with me? Is there something wrong with my version of love?

I wanted to know the reasons!

I couldn't stop rewinding these thoughts in my head over and over and over again. It was horrible. My ex actually told me repeatedly, "Noah, seriously, you have to calm down.

We obviously wanted to go in different directions with our lives."

This was absolutely true. It was totally factual that we wanted different things out of life. There was a legitimate and obvious discrepancy about how we wanted to live.

But I couldn't get over it.

And this led me to being concretely rude to the people around me. I acted nuts everyday. Instead of enjoying the new place I was living, I wouldn't stop talking about my ex. Instead of finding a new job and getting on with my life, I was dwelling on my ex. When people tried to bring me places to have a good time, I would end up talking about my ex. I even went on dates with very friendly people and instead of enjoying the date, I talked about my ex.

I was like some ideologue or someone in a cult, but instead of being obsessed with politics or my crazy religion, I was obsessed with my ex. I had turned her into a mythology, a religion, a political platform. I was super annoying.

It was like I had turned the world into two discriminations. There was the world in which

I got to think about my ex and talk about my ex, and this world was good and comfortable to live in. Then there was the world that was not my ex, which was a bad, boring world that I had no interest in.

It was horrible. I was demanding that the people around me, the people that love and care about me, deal with me not as the person they once knew, but this crazed ideologue obsessed with his ex.

But this scenario can happen in many different ways: Say a mother has three children. One of them dies young, and the mother loses it, gets extremely depressed for years, and neglects her other two children. Or a person goes to war and experiences horrible violence, then goes back to their family and has terrible PTSD. They end up neglecting or even terrorizing their family. Or a woman has several children with a man, then the man she loved leaves her, and the woman tortures her children for decades because of this past betrayal.

There is no winning in clinging to the past.

Who wins when you won't give yourself to the present? No one.

But we shouldn't forget the microcosm.

If a friend needs five dollars give it to them and then forget it. Dwelling on those five dollars, where will it lead?

If your coworker is having a bad day and they tell you to "fuck off," just forget it. The next time you see them, pretend it didn't happen. Of course, they will be worried that you are mad, but if you don't mention it, it will allow everyone to peacefully forget it even happened.

Just forget everything. Always be in a state of forgetting.

I think the phrase is "don't look back."

Participation.

We have to understand that as we are experiencing events, other people, animals, and plants, they are experiencing us.

We are being experienced.

If you're depressed, find someone, anyone, and make them happy. Buy them their favorite drink, bring them to a movie, call them on the phone, do something for or with someone else.

Participate in the flux of humanity.

Our lives are made up of experiences, so

have fun experiences. Help create an atmosphere where people are having a good time.

Pet your cat. Participate in the life of your cat.

Play fetch with your dog.

Weed your garden.

Mow your grass.

Clean your refrigerator.

You are depressed because you are trapped in your head. You think for some reason that your mental chatterbox is more relevant than the people and things around you. The chatter of your mind is exactly that: nothing but chatter. It is better to clean your car than to listen to every crazy thought bouncing about in your head.

Mindfulness.

The opposite of mindfulness is being mindless.

The weird thing is that, when we are mindless, that is when our mental chatterbox is overwhelming us, when our thoughts are bouncing around, when we are dwelling on a past we refuse to forget, or chasing after a future we never catch up with.

Mindless people don't care about other people. They only care about their own thoughts.

Mindless people can't control their thoughts. That is why they are mindless. Only when we have control do we have a mind.

It is fun to be mindful. When we eat, we chew slowly, we feel the food in our mouths, we taste the food. When we hike through a forest, we breathe deeply. Instead of racing to the top, we look at trees, we feel the bumpy trail beneath our feet, we watch a deer run by.

When we are having fun with the people we care about, we are mindful of their needs, we pay attention to them, we don't demand that they conform to our ideas about life. We accept the people around us and let them be. We enjoy them for what they are.

Being mindful is living in the now.

The now is the safest place to be.

No horrible memories of the past.

No worries of the future.

Just the now. If you let yourself live in the now, it almost feels like a magical island in the ocean where everything glows, undulates, vibrates.

People throughout history have often painted pictures of people alone on a boat out in the ocean in terrible storms. But those are the people who demand. The person in the boat wants the storm to end. They are angry and frustrated that they chose to go out on a day with a storm and they are angry at the storm for existing. The mindful person instead says, "Oh wow, a storm, either I will die or have one of the coolest experiences of my life. Let's see what happens."

We always have a choice in tough situations.

We can scream, "no, no, no," or we can say, "I'm going to do the best I can."

Being mindful is about saying "yes" to the now.

Being mindful is about paying close attention to the people, animals, and plants around you in order to see what support they need.

Being mindful is about not paying attention to the mental chatter and instead enjoying the sounds of bugs in a forest.

You can access the now anytime you want. Just breathe. Scan the world you live in. Utilize your different senses. Focus on your sense of touch and feeling. Focus on your sense of smell. Listen to the sounds, but don't name them.

Just say, "I don't know."

Just exist, as everything else is existing.

But to go further with this idea of being experienced, and how important your participation in the flux of humanity is:

An extreme example first. I've known people in my life who got molested when they were children by adults in their life. Those people I can tell have extreme PTSD, extreme anxiety, extreme issues with fear, extreme issues with anger and commitment. And it never ends their whole life. The pain of the molestation never ends. Through one act, a human being can ruin many days of another human's life.

But the opposite is true also. If you are kind to someone, if you help them and talk to them without judgment, they will also remember that their entire lives.

Say you encounter a homeless person who has to sleep out in the cold at night, and you give that homeless person a sleeping bag to sleep in. When that homeless person is warm at night because of what you chose to do, that warmth is you.

If you give someone a book to read, and they enjoy it, that enjoyment is you.

If you give someone a pair of socks, and they love how the socks look and feel on their feet, you are those feelings.

You have so much power, but all you want to do is entertain yourself and listen to your mental chatter.

Meditation.

It doesn't seem possible to get anywhere without meditation.

I think many novelists and philosophers in Western Culture were able to attain some sense of enlightenment because they were extreme introverts, they spent many hours alone, or they traveled extensively which lead to a realization of some sort.

However, Buddhism recognized that the easiest way to figure out that our minds are just chatterboxes is by sitting and staring at a wall. By sitting quietly we come to see, internally feel, notice, and recognize that many of the thoughts we have, many of the feelings we have, and many of our instantaneous reactions are nothing but passing mirages.

I understand that this is hard to realize. We are all raised with the idea we should be busy, that we should be bettering ourselves, that we need to have and protect certain things, that our identities are so important. Really, these things aren't true.

Yoga can teach this too. There is nothing like being in yoga class, doing weird stretches that seem to last forever. It all seems so pointless, and that is the point: to engage in the pointless, to learn the futility of human existence.

Several times in my life I have put a massive amount of effort into something and ended up with nothing. I dated a person for seven years, and I haven't seen her face in years. I went to college and never found a well paying job.

We have all done so much work, we have all put in so much effort, we have all spent so many hours looking for a job, we have all tried and tried at things, and then we have watched them fail.

But that is what life is.

A futile experiment lived out by each organism.

There is nowhere to go.

As Samuel Beckett said in *Waiting for Godot*, "Nothing to be done."

As Dogen said in the Genjo Koan, "A fish swims in the ocean, and no matter how far it swims there is no end to the water."

You keep existing until you don't exist anymore.

Walking from one room to another room, talking to this person, talking to that person, feeling these feelings, feeling those feelings, having this mood, having that mood, feeling rain, feeling wind, hearing music, hearing the sounds of children playing, looking at trees, looking at cars, falling in love, having a nice dinner, arguing, laughing, being disgruntled, being calm. Being being being.

Hiking taught me this.

But you have to lose the goal of getting to the end of the trail.

Of getting to the end of the trail at a specific time.

When you are on the trail, whether it be the beginning, middle, or end of the trail, you are on the mountain, you are in the canyon.

If you are on the trail, you are on the trail.

Feel your feet hit the rocks and soil, touch leaves as you pass by them, touch rocks, just breathe, relax, there is no need to worry about getting to the end of the trail.

If you don't feel like finishing the trail, there is no need to finish.

The trail is the trail.

Who are you trying to impress?

People in my life have asked to hike with me who don't usually hike. They know I hike. I post pictures of it on Facebook. When people ask me what I plan on doing next week, I notify them I am going hiking. They will ask me to go hiking. They feel that it would be fun to hike, that it would be exciting and relaxing to be in the forest or desert on their day off. But then these weird pressures happen. They want to wake up at 5 a.m. and then get breakfast. They have to see the sunrise. They have to go to the store and buy expensive hiking gear. They worry about things like snakes and mountain lions. They are more concerned with the time-share cabins on the way to the trailhead. They want to know how much the time-share cabins cost. It is like they are compelled to talk about money even though they are in nature. Then, when they get on the trail, they want to be the first to get to the end of the trail. They want to make sure you think they are a good hiker. They want everything but to enjoy the trail.

I'm sure there are also people in Buddhism and yoga classes that instead of just staring at the wall are actually telling themselves, "I'm staring, I'm meditating, look at me I'm meditating, I'm so spiritual. The rest of the world is not as spiritual as I am. I hate the world because they are not as spiritual as I am. Look at me. I can meditate for longer periods of time than the person next to me. I can see that they are scratching their leg. They can't maintain their pose like I can. I've read these Buddhist books, and they haven't. I am a better Buddhist. Look at me. I'm spiritual."

The yoga person thinks, "Everyone is looking at me, I am so good at yoga, I can do all these positions, I once learned yoga in India." But mostly I've heard, "Everyone can see I'm overweight in these tight clothes. I can't maintain this pose. People can see I have trouble holding poses. I feel so sick from the heat and exercise, but I can't show people I'm sick. I will remain sick and keep holding these poses."

Just let it all go. Give up.

Stop trying.

Stop putting pressure on yourself to be anything.

If you hear your mind making these thoughts, if you feel these feelings, scream at your mind and body, "No more! I will not participate in these absurd pressures and ideas anymore."

If you want to hike to the top of the mountain, take one step at a time. If you take one step at a time, the end of the trail will arrive.

Don't walk to the end of the trail.

Take one step at a time.

Self-Reflection.

It seems weird to think, but a lot of people never self-reflect. They never bother for even a few minutes to take a walk and think deeply about the logic of their life, about the logic of their government, of their culture, or even why they have made the choices they have made.

It just never happens for a lot of people.

What do people do then? How are they operating?

Of course everyone "feels things." Everyone has fears, attachments, compulsions, anxiety, loneliness, etc. We are all basically having the same fundamental human experience, but when doubts arise, when bad feelings come, some people just shove them down or have no ability to articulate those feelings because they have never had experience with ideas that might help them articulate their feelings.

That is mostly what people do. They have feelings, and then they project those feelings onto the things, people, and texts they encounter. If a person is driven by power, the powerful God will appeal to them. If a person feels hurt and like the world dislikes them, the parts about slaves and Jesus will appeal to them. If a person feel a great amount of resentment, *Revelation* might appeal to them.

This can be done with any text or philosophy.

Even though a lot of people never have moments of self-reflection, it doesn't mean they aren't feeling deep things. Many great musicians in history have had zero ability to verbally articulate complex ideas, but if you hand them a saxophone or a guitar, boom, you know deep complex feelings are happening in their subconscious.

My friend is a very articulate, well-read, worldly person who has a doctorate and knows three languages.

She said to me, "My mother wants me to visit her all the time, but she never really asks me about what I do. I want her to ask me about what I do."

I replied, "She just wants you in the room. She watched you grow up. She gave birth to you. She has deep feelings concerning your existence. She wants your existence near her. It has nothing to do with language. It is ineffable. It is wordless what she feels. She just feels it."

Just because someone can't articulate what they are feeling doesn't mean they don't have tremendous feelings and complex emotions for what is happening.

Even if you have the deep ability for self-reflection and articulation, it doesn't mean other people aren't feeling. Use your abilities to help them, not to justify your existence as more important than theirs.

But what is self-reflection?

Self-reflection is trying to understand oneself, how you operate.

Self-reflection is trying to understand other people, how they operate.

I say "trying" because self-reflection is never perfect. Something always remains inexplicable. It seems like a lot of people hope that when they die, a heavenly being explains the meaning of everything. Even if that was something that would happen, that's not how our reality works now. In our current reality, we can never completely figure out why one person said that, and why this person did that, why we like broccoli and our sibling likes asparagus. Most of the time, those specifics mean nothing. We can all maintain shelter and get food without knowing the specifics of our psychologies. Animals and plants live, experience life, and die without ever writing books of religion and philosophy.

To self-reflect means to figure out how you tick, what causes you to react with sadness, what causes you to react with excitement, what causes you to react with fear or anger.

A simple thing to do would be:

After you react with anger over something, take a walk.

Think about what happened. List the chain of events in your head. Write them down, if you want to. Think about your mood previous to the anger. See the events in your head, tie them together in context, see where the anger started, find that specific second when you went from happiness to sudden anger. Stare at the moment of anger. Feel the anger. Most likely, you will realize your nature, the roots of moods.

Anger never leads to happiness.

An eye for an eye is stupid because more anger leads nowhere.

Seriously reflect. Has being angry ever lead to being happy?

Anger only leads to more anger.

Being mean or unethical never leads to happiness.

We all know that sometimes, even when we have good intentions, things can turn out badly, but when people know you've done something with good intentions, people forget the harm more quickly.

Examples: I once lived in a town that had two giant truck stops on top of a hill. The city officials zoned the truck stops with the good intentions of bringing business to the area, which would lead to job growth and more tax dollars for the local schools. These were all good intentions. The city officials did not realize that the hill would be completely covered in cement and what that would imply is that when a hard rain came the water would have nowhere to go. That spring the rains flooded the businesses at the bottom of the hill. But the people never got mad about this. They forgave the city officials and fixed things so buildings wouldn't get flooded again.

Concerning bad intentions: If a government imprisons journalists for reporting news that goes against the elite government and wealthy classes with only the intention of self-protection, people don't forget that. People will complain about that for years. Unethical behavior only leads to resistance, rebellion, and disgrace. Cruelty only leads to more anger and more problems.

If you accidentally wreck your partner's car, even though something very bad has happened but you obviously did it with no malice, you will probably be forgiven. You might even laugh about it.

But if you cheat on your partner and then leave a condom in their car and they find it, well, trouble is going to arise. You've done something out of selfishness, maybe even malice.

Doing things with good intentions pragmatically works out better because if things get messed up, people more easily forgive, but if you do things with resentment, anger, and your own selfishness as your goal, then people are less likely to forget. Instead, they give resistance and retaliation. This is an argument against Ayn Randism.

Anger and selfish intentions lead only to more anger and trouble.

Self-reflection is about realizing one's place in the scheme of things, realizing how you arise from the world, about how other people exist in the scheme of things, and how they arise from the world.

Self-reflection is trying to find out what will make you enthusiastic and excited to be alive, meanwhile separating the things you are doing because of social and subconscious pressures.

Self-reflection can also help us against resentment and self-righteousness. When we feel the ugly emotion of resentment arise in us, we have to confront it. Don't hide from your ugliness. Face it.

When you feel resentment and jealousy, take a walk alone. Let that emotion come. Let those horrible thoughts come, dissect them, pick them apart, figure them out. If you let resentment grow it becomes self-righteousness.

Resentment leads to saying "no" irrationally or without thought, and this leads to self-righteousness. You begin rigidly defining your reality: this is this and that is that, I am this and you are that.

This strict definition of reality creates self-righteousness. You become a world of "dos" and "don'ts." Eventually the "dos" and the "don'ts" control you, and you have landed in a reality of delusion and mental slavery. You begin putting pressure on yourself to "do" and to "don't." You begin to hate those who are different than you. Resentment doesn't lead to happiness, it leads to irrational fear, paranoia, and hate.

Learn your resentment. Study your pain. If you want pain to end, you have to study it. Do it while you can. If you are lucky, you can figure out why you suffer so much by the time you're forty. Then you still have years to live that are at least mostly free of needless pressure, fear, paranoia, self-loathing, and frustrations over the trivial.

If you stop saying "no," if you stop forcing a bunch of "dos" and "don'ts" on your Dasein, on your Being, you will enter into the ineffable.

Yoda was wrong.
There is no "try."
There is no "do."
There is no "don't."
Don't "do" and don't not "do."
Give up doing.
Let yourself exist.
Let yourself interact.
Let yourself arise as all things arise.

Justifications.

There is nothing more troublesome than justifying oneself.

Give up justifying your life.

We do a million things to justify our lives. We go to school, we get good grades, we perform at high levels. We work endlessly to impress our teachers and coaches. We grow up and go to college, learn a trade, go to the military, get married. We have kids, we buy expensive cars, we buy houses we can't afford; we buy an endless assortment of crap because we think it makes us look better.

We build empires around us to make ourselves look justified.

I have known people so consumed with pride and self-justification that they take jobs that sound good even though they are in locations they hate.

I have known people who stay married even though they hate their partners.

I have known people who went to the best schools and still feel depressed because they didn't go to a better school.

North Americans are obsessed with justifying their lives, with not being looked at as someone who wastes their life, as a person who couldn't capture the dream of capitalism.

What is there to win with pride?

What is there to win with an endless psychological need to impress the people around you?

When you spend your life impressing other people, where are you?

There is no *you*.

When you are driven to impress, it is all about other people and their expectations.

Where is your song? Where is your music? For the person who is obsessed with impression, there is only justification, there is only the future possibility of impression and justification.

There is no now for those who live for impression.

Concerning personal relations:

We encounter something that intimidates us: it could be a person, it could be rock climbing, or a rattlesnake.

What do we do? What is our usual reaction?

We feel insecure, we begin to panic inside, our heart rushes, our chest aches.

We begin to feel anxiety. When we are intimidated, we lose our footing. The floor beneath us cracks open and we fall through. As Heidegger noted, we are *falling*. And we desperately want to gain footing again. We want to reclaim our position and feel normal and strong.

This is where the justification starts.

If we are dealing with someone who makes us feel small, unintelligent, or weak, we might belittle them. Maybe I'm in a doctor's office waiting room and someone says, "these doctors don't know anything." The person obviously feels intimidated by the doctor and wants to bring the doctor down to their level.

(It should be noted, the doctor might not even care. The doctor might have become a doctor because their parents scolded them until they became a doctor. They really wanted to be a high school music teacher, and in reality the doctor hates their life and doesn't care about the intelligence level of their patients at all. Or the doctor has worked endlessly to become a doctor because they are consumed with compassion for other humans, desperately want to make their fellow humans feel healthy and strong, and can't stand the sight of physical misery in other people. We often project intimidation on someone who doesn't even care about intimidating anyone.)

Belittling is a form of bringing someone else down.

Most of our harsh talk is belittling. It doesn't matter if it is about the boss, politicians, or movie directors. When we immediately dismiss someone, we are belittling.

"Those politicians are idiots."

"Their music sucks. It is so corporate."

"I don't eat crickets. They're gross."

"I hate his writing. Everyone who likes his books is an idiot."

"She is good at guitar, but she's fat."

Those aren't factual statements. No one is trying to understand anything in those types of comments. There is no nuance. There is nothing that gives reasons or motivations. There is only belittlement, only vague justifications to liquidate shame and feed one's resentment.

More examples:

You are talking with a lawyer, and even though it has nothing to do with the context, you bring up the fact you went to college just to remind the lawyer that you are educated too.

Or a nurse goes to the doctor and immediately announces to the doctor, "I'm a nurse, and this is what I think." Because they want the doctor to know their status.

For me, and I think for a lot of people, we have the habit of justifying our lives to our parents. Our parents put demands on us. Sometimes we don't live up to those demands, and we begin to justify our lives, finding scapegoats instead of the truth.

Justifications are hardly ever true or needed. We create them because we are panicked and we want to feel calm again.

Justifications can get even worse. They can really tear us apart. We can begin looking at everything nicer than what we have. We can become obsessed with nice things and people who have more talent than us, or people who are willing to put more effort into things than we do. This will only lead to self-loathing.

When we want justice for everyone, there is peace in that. There is harmony in that. When we want the rules to be the same for everyone, there is unity of humankind. There is an understanding that we all fundamentally operate the same way.

When we justify ourselves out of jealousy, then there is only "me."

When there is only "me," then you're alone against everyone else.

When you panic and begin to justify yourself, listen to yourself, study how and why you justify yourself.

If you are scared just say it. "I am scared." It is okay to be scared.

Let yourself be honest and open. Now watch. Humans can be really friendly. They have to be given the chance.

Instead of justifying yourself, do nothing.

Lin Chi said, "As long as you seek something it can only lead to suffering. Better to do nothing."

Do nothing.

If you want to get really good at life, do nothing.

Do nothing, even when doing something.

Just have fun.

Fun is doing nothing.

When you are at work, do nothing.

When you are at home, do nothing.
When you are making love, do nothing.
There is nothing to be done.
Nowhere to go.
Nothing to do.
When you look at a dog, it seems to be doing nothing.
When a dog looks at you, you seem to be doing nothing.
You are doing nothing and assuming you are doing everything. And that's your problem.
You were doing nothing the whole time.
Your whole life was nothing but you walking around, lying on couches, eating food and chatting about little trivialities.
And you took it all so seriously.
Do nothing.
Put your chips down. Place the bet.

Pascal's Wager in Another Way

We can also use Pascal's Wager to answer life's dilemmas.

My friend said to me, "Should I go to grad school? I will have to take out $40,000 in student loans."

I responded, "If there is a God, do you think God cares if you ever pay back your student loans? If there is no God, then student loans mean nothing. What matters is that you go to the college, work hard, and are friendly to the people around you."

Another person I know from Europe visited America and met someone and fell in love.

She asked, "Should I just forget my love and go back to Europe? It is going to be hard dealing with the embassy and all the paperwork?"

I responded, "If there is a God, then God brought you to that person. If there is no God, live where you want, but remain friendly and mindful to the people around you."

Another person asked, "Should I hate myself because I have failed to attain a prestigious position in society?"

Another person asked a similar question, "Should I hate myself? I have attained a prestigious position in society, but I have not attained wealth."

I responded, "If there is a God, God probably doesn't care about your job title or bank balance. And if there is no God, then your job title/bank balance are just extremely transitory events and mean nothing. Go watch a movie with a friend and calm down."

Another question posed: "I don't like people. I think they are stupid, unjust, and rude. Should I resign myself and live quietly going to work and doing my personal thing, or should I write articles, protest, and do things to halt the injustice and create a better world?"

I responded, "If there is a God, if you follow the maxims of Kant and Shantideva and make an honest attempt at positively participating in the events of the world, I believe God would see beauty in that. If there is no God, you still have to recognize we are as humans are all living together, sharing the same planet, and it is wise to crave justice because you need justice just as everyone needs justice."

11.
Near Death Experiences

The common opinions on near death experiences are that they are one of two things: the first of these is that they are truly mystical experiences in which our heart stops and we slip out of our bodies. Then we go through a white light and enter into an alternate dimension. The second thing a near death experience could indicate is that our brains create a dream by sending peaceful chemicals through our body. We feel drugged and peacefully mentally recede from existence.

I feel fine with near death experiences being scientific or mystical. Of course, what choice do I have in the matter?

It is fun to think about though. We die and a beautiful white light appears. We rise out of our bodies and float like birds. We've always felt so jealous of birds and their ability of flight, and now we just feel incredibly excited at the feeling of floating out of our bodies.

We look around the earth one last time thinking, "What a funny place."

We enter this white light, Pristine Cognition, as the Tibetan Buddhists call it.

We go through the white light and see those who have died before us. Maybe we see our father, a neighbor, a friend from high school taken early in life, maybe a professor or our partner.

There they are, the dead before us.

One of them comes forward. We know which one. We all know who we would pick to speak to us at this moment of oddness.

They come forward and say, "You did it, just like we did it. What do you know now?"

We feel puzzled for a second and say, "There is no difference between learning to walk and learning to die. The first thing I learned and the last thing I learned are the same."

The person smiles. Then those who have died before walk forward and shake your hand. They hug you and say, "You've done it, you've done it."

Then it hits you. There was no duality the whole time. It wasn't me versus the universe. The whole universe was nothing but different shaped things made of the same substance wiggling around, being born, experiencing, growing old, and receding from existence to make room for new forms to experience and recede in the same way. It didn't matter if you were a giant star, a bear in a forest, a Muslim in Saudi Arabia, a Christian in Denmark, a rattlesnake in a desert, a maple tree in Canada, a capuchin monkey in Costa Rica, millions of cicadas humming in Korea, every blade of wheat in Nebraska, or a writer in Las Vegas. It was all the same. It was just your mind telling you things were different.

Those who died before you say, "Did you get *it*?"

You smile and fade out.

Noah Cicero was born in a field in Ohio. He had an unhappy childhood in a town with one red light, one convenience store, and several churches. To tolerate reality he would take long walks in the forest behind his house. In the forest he could think. The trees did not judge him. When Noah Cicero was 15 years old, he started liking books. His high school principal gave him copies of Emerson's *Self-Reliance* and Thoreau's *Walden*. At the age of 23, after a trip to the mental ward, Noah Cicero wrote The Human War, which has been made into a movie and translated many times. Since then, he has written many books of fiction, traveled to 43 states, lived in Asia, and traveled to South America. Noah Cicero has never been to Europe. He thinks this defines him in some way. After a traumatic incident in 2013, Noah Cicero lost his mind. He had what would one would call a nervous breakdown. He was trapped, snowed in on a mountain in the forest of Oregon, with nothing but a copy of Bodhidharma's Teachings. After reading Bodhidharma, Noah Cicero dropped to his knees and said "Thank you, Hashem."

www.ingramcontent.com/pod-product-compliance
Lightning Source LLC
Chambersburg PA
CBHW050537300426
44113CB00012B/2138